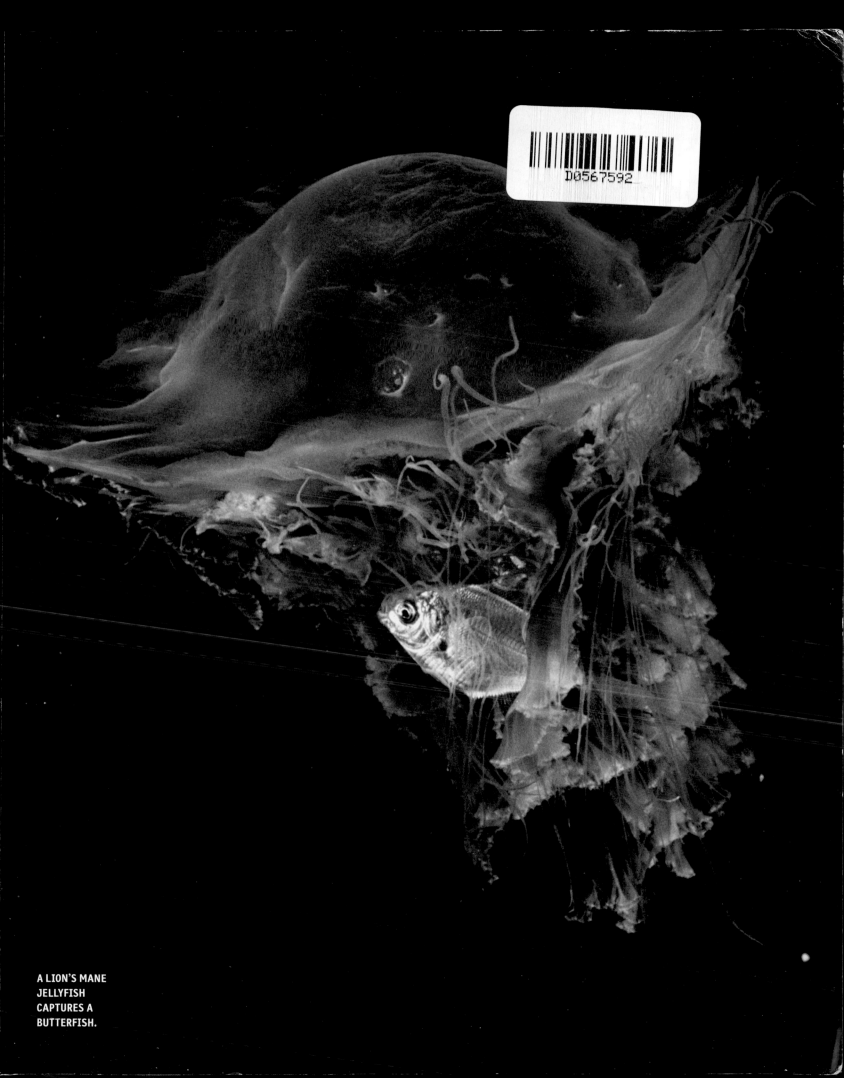

A LION'S MANE
JELLYFISH
CAPTURES A
BUTTERFISH.

THE WASP LARVA ATTACHED TO THIS SPIDER SUCKS THE SPIDER'S BODY FLUIDS. THE ZOMBIFIED SPIDER THEN TEARS DOWN ITS OWN WEB AND BUILDS A NEW ONE THAT PROTECTS THE LARVA'S COCOON FROM PREDATORS.

ANIMAL ZOMBIES!

AND OTHER BLOODSUCKING BEASTS, CREEPY CREATURES, AND REAL-LIFE MONSTERS

CHANA STIEFEL

NATIONAL GEOGRAPHIC
WASHINGTON, D.C.

CONTENTS

ZOMBIE ROACH,
PAGE 10

TAWNY FROGMOUTH,
PAGE 85

THIS ANT WAS INFECTED BY A MIND-CONTROLLING FUNGUS.

DEAR BRAVE READER,

BEWARE! You are about to enter the darkest, creepiest corners of our world. You'll collide with creatures that **INVADE BRAINS, DRINK BLOOD,** and even **DEVOUR THEIR OWN MOMS!** You'll confront howlers, prowlers, and foul flesh-eaters. You'll brush up against critters with **NEEDLELIKE FANGS** and **TOXIC TENTACLES.** These "monsters" dwell in the gloomiest jungles and the deepest seas. Some tiny creatures may also lurk **UNDER YOUR MATTRESS** and even **CLING TO YOUR EYELASHES.**

But know this: These creatures never intend to do you harm. It's a critter-eat-critter world, and the creepy animals on these pages have adapted all kinds of **HAIR-RAISING TECHNIQUES TO SURVIVE** and pass on their genes. After **THREE BILLION YEARS OF EVOLUTION,** these "beasts" have developed extreme powers to fight off predators, adapt to habitat destruction, and resist chemicals invading their environment. Scientists still do not understand the unique role that many species play in the great web of life. So tread lightly as you explore **NATURE'S HAUNTED HOUSE.** In the end (if you leave unscathed), you might go from **"YIKES"** to **"LIKES"** for the crafty, spine-tingling wonders that surround you.

NOW TURN THE PAGE ...
IF YOU DARE!

CHAPTER 1

THE LIVING DEAD

ZOMBIE ZONE

In horror stories, zombies can range from "the living dead"—animated corpses—to people whose brains have been taken over by killer viruses. With dark circles under their eyes, zombies appear numb and dazed, stomping through town while scavenging for their next "brainy" meal. *Mmmmm, nom nom nom!*

Along the way, their victims often become zombies, too. Before you know it, it's a full-scale zombie apocalypse!

Luckily, zombies are just a myth ... or are they? Scientists have found that in nature, real "zombies" do exist! Scientists have long known that parasites—organisms that live on or inside other creatures—have the ability to take command of their host. But researchers only recently discovered *how* parasites craftily turn their hosts into "zombies." Your eyes may bug out as you explore the latest discoveries of wasps, worms, and many other creatures that invade the brains of their hosts and manipulate them to do their bidding. But rest assured, there is a happy ending. You'll soon discover how the living dead play an essential role in the circle of life.

THIS FROG WAS DEFORMED BY INVADING FLATWORMS, MAKING IT EASY PREY FOR BIRDS.

BRAINWASHED LADYBUG

THE TINY FEMALE PARASITIC WASP *DINOCAMPUS COCCI-NELLAE* **LOOKS PRETTY HARMLESS,** because she's only about the size of an ice-cream sprinkle! But get ready ...

ZOMBIFICATION

When she's ready to lay an egg, the wasp doesn't just build a nice, cozy nest. Instead, she flies over to an unassuming ladybug, stings it in the belly, and injects an egg (1). Yikes!

The wasp's life cycle—a process known as metamorphosis—actually begins *inside* the body of another species! Within the living ladybug, the wasp egg hatches and a larva, the immature wormlike form of an insect, emerges. The wasp larva begins to devour its host's internal organs. On the outside, the ladybug appears perfectly normal, and it will go about its buggy business for about three weeks, *until* ...

... the larva chews a hole in the ladybug's exoskeleton (its outer shell) and wriggles out (2)! But the ladybug still isn't free to fly away. The wasp larva then ensnares the ladybug as its own personal bodyguard!

IT'S **NOT OVER** YET

The larva then spins a silk cocoon around itself right between the ladybug's legs (3). For a week, the brainwashed ladybug will be the cocoon's bodyguard as the larva transforms into an immature wasp, or pupa, inside the cocoon. The zombified ladybug even protects the pupa from predators as it develops into an adult wasp. When a hungry insect gets too close to the cocoon, the ladybug shakes its limbs and chases it away! Soon an adult wasp emerges from the cocoon and flies away, leaving the ladybug to either recover or die. Unfortunately for them, ladybugs that survive this ordeal are sometimes attacked again—and the zombie cycle repeats!

A PARASITIC WASP SPINS ITS COCOON BETWEEN THE LEGS OF A SPOTTED LADYBUG.

BY THE NUMBERS

About **25 percent** of zombified ladybugs **recover** after the wasp larvae they protect mature and fly away.

9

DID YOU KNOW?

As if performing precise brain surgery, the jewel wasp snakes its stinger through the cockroach's brain to find the part that controls movement.

ZOMBIE
ROACH

MEET THE MONSTER

DON'T BE FOOLED BY ITS SHIMMERY COLORS. The parasitic emerald jewel wasp, *Ampulex compressa*, is a master manipulator. Although many wasps paralyze their prey for food, this pretty wasp has a more "monstrous" plan. It injects venom into an unsuspecting cockroach. Then it commandeers the roach to do its bidding.

BY THE NUMBERS

The cockroach victim can be **six times the size** of the invading wasp.

ZOMBIFICATION

THE WASP STINGS THE ROACH IN THE THORAX.

First the wasp stings the roach's thorax, the middle section of the roach's body between its front legs, to temporarily paralyze the bug so it can't fight back. Then the wasp injects venom directly into the roach's brain. The venom blocks a chemical that controls the cockroach's will to skitter away. The roach can no longer control its own movement ... but the wasp can!

To regain some energy (hey, this zombie business is *exhausting*), the wasp chomps off one of the zombified roach's antennae. From the oozing wound, the wasp then sips the roach's hemolymph, the insect version of blood, which is packed with sugars and proteins. Next the wasp grabs the stump of one of the roach's antennae and pulls it toward a burrow like a puppet master pulling the strings of a marionette. The zombie roach is completely helpless. The wasp then lays an egg on the roach's abdomen. To keep predators away, the clever wasp seals the burrow with pebbles. Then it flies off to look for its next victim.

IT'S NOT OVER YET

The mindless roach now acts like a wasp-egg incubator. About two days later, the egg hatches, but the newborn larva shows no gratitude to its cockroach host. Instead, the larva punches a hole in the roach's exoskeleton and proceeds to eat the roach alive! Slowly, over several days, it devours the roach's internal organs. The larva then forms a cocoon inside the hollow shell of the dead roach.

After about a month, an adult wasp emerges from the roach's shell (its roach motel, if you will). It finds its way out of the burrow and flies away, ready to mate ... and hunt down another roach!

•••• HORROR OR HELPER? ••••

Not only are cockroaches **CREEPY CRITTERS,** but they also have **harmful bacteria** living inside them: microbes that can harm the invading wasp larvae. To keep its meal **fresh** and stave off infection from the killer bacteria, the hungry larva smears an **antibiotic cocktail** on the roach's inner body. These antibiotics produced by the jewel wasp are **NEW TO SCIENCE.** Scientists may explore them further to see if they are valuable in producing new medicines.

NATURE PHOTOGRAPHER ANAND VARMA

ANAND TAKES A SELFIE ON LOCATION IN ECUADOR.

Growing up in Atlanta, Georgia, U.S.A., Anand Varma spent a lot of time poking around outdoors. He couldn't have imagined that one day he would be traveling around the world as a professional nature photographer and taking pictures of all kinds of wild critters, including animal "zombies"!

Varma first picked up a camera during high school. Shooting pictures became his hobby, but his true passion was science. While studying biology at the University of California, Berkeley, Varma's instructor asked if he would be interested in working as an assistant to a National Geographic photographer named David Liittschwager. "I thought it would be a two-week commitment," Varma said. It turned out to be a life-changing experience. He spent the next seven years under Liittschwager's wing, traveling and learning the ropes of nature photography.

Recently, a college friend who is a parasitologist (a scientist who studies parasites and their hosts)

suggested that Varma photograph the mind-controlling creatures. He was soon in zombie zone.

But the assignment proved to be extremely challenging. Parasites often live inside their hosts, they tend to be tiny, and they don't exactly pose for the camera. When Varma was photographing a

ANAND USES A HIGH-SPEED CAMERA TO PHOTOGRAPH BEES IN FLIGHT.

hairworm that had invaded a cricket, for example, the worm kept wriggling out of the cricket's behind before Varma could snap a shot. "Even the humidity of your hand or your breath could be enough to make the worm go shooting out of the cricket," Varma said. "I had to try over and over again." He eventually discovered that if he cooled the crickets in

the fridge, he could slow down the process and get his shot.

Then there was location. He photographed some species that were infected in labs, but others he could capture only in the rain forest, like zombified ants in Brazil. In Costa Rica, where he photographed zombie spiders, he set up a studio in his hotel room and put a "Do Not Disturb" sign on his door. And Varma photographed worm-infested crickets in his own kitchen!

Varma also learned a few creative tricks along the way. "People's eyes don't usually light up when you tell them about parasites," he said. "Their usual reaction is, 'That's gross.'" To keep people captivated, he uses techniques that he picked up from reading graphic novels and watching films and Japanese animation. He invented new lighting methods using hair-thin tubes called fiber optics to direct light and make hosts, like the crickets, appear in silhouette, while shining the spotlight on the invading worms. Suddenly, the "gross" looks mysteriously beautiful.

THIS ZOMBIFIED MALE SHEEP CRAB HAS BECOME A HATCHERY FOR BARNACLE EGGS. NURTURED BY THE CRAB, THOUSANDS OF BABY BARNACLES (THE DOTS ON THIS PAGE) HATCH AND SPREAD OUT TO INVADE OTHER CRABS.

A "ZOMBIE" LADYBUG PROTECTS A WASP'S COCOON.

A CRUSTACEAN IS INFECTED BY A PARASITIC WORM.

CONTROLLED CRICKETS

MEET THE MONSTER

HAIRWORMS ARE PARASITES THAT LIVE ON LAND BUT NEED TO BREED IN WATER. How do they get there? It's not as simple as throwing on a bathing suit and diving in. Instead, hairworms commandeer crickets! Crickets normally avoid bodies of water because of fishy predators. But zombifying hairworms know some mind-control tricks to get crickets to do their bidding!

ZOMBIFICATION

Hairworms aren't normally on a cricket's menu. Instead, a hairworm larva might be eaten by a mosquito, a critter more likely to end up on a cricket's dinner plate. Once it's eaten, a hairworm grows inside the new host's body. Then the larva pumps a toxic brew of mind-controlling chemicals into the cricket that cause it to dive right into the deep end. Sensing the splash, the hairworm, which can grow up to a foot (30 cm) long, then wriggles out of the cricket's rear end and swims away to mate. It looks like a swimming strand of thin spaghetti.

But how does a hairworm larva get into a mosquito? When a female hairworm lays eggs in the water, they sink to the bottom. The hatched larvae can't swim. Eventually the larvae of other insects living in the water, like mosquitoes, eat the hairworm larvae. When the insect larvae grow into adult mosquitoes, they fly away with the hairworm larvae on board. A hungry cricket eats one of the hairworm-infested mosquitoes ... and the zombie cycle hits replay.

DID YOU KNOW?

Hairworms don't have mouths. They absorb nutrients from their host right through their skin.

BY THE NUMBERS

Scientists have discovered about **350 species of hairworms.** One species of hairworm can grow up to **six feet (1.8 m) long!** A female hairworm can lay as many as **15 million eggs!**

HORROR OR HELPER?

Scientists have a **WORKING THEORY** about how the hairworm's chemicals cause a cricket to **move toward water:** Because bodies of water **REFLECT MOONLIGHT**, the **cricket is attracted to the moon's glimmer** on lakes and streams. But the hairworm's crazy chemicals may cause the insect to become so **dazzled** that it takes a deadly dive into the water. Scientists are exploring the biochemical pathways in which parasites, like hairworms, **MANIPULATE THE BRAIN** of their host. They are hoping their discoveries help researchers find **new medicines or vaccines.**

ZOMBIE CYCLES

MEET THE MONSTER

AN ADULT LANCET LIVER FLUKE (A TYPE OF FLATWORM) HAS AN UNUSUAL HOME: It lives inside the liver of a grazing cow. The fluke's eggs take a ride to the great outdoors when the cow poops in a field. An unsuspecting snail then comes along and nibbles on the poop and eggs. When the eggs hatch inside the snail, the snail forms a protective capsule (called a cyst) around the eggs and then ejects them by coughing them up in balls of mucus.

ZOMBIFICATION

Hang on, zombie fans, there's more! An ant comes along and eats the fluke-filled slime balls. The fluke sneaks into the ant's brain and turns it into a real-life zombie—forcing it to climb to the tippy top of a blade of grass, where it sits, frozen, until a grazing cow comes along.

"Moo! What's this?" The cow chows down on a delicious blade of grass with—crunch!—a liver fluke and ant topping. The cow eats the fluke-ant snack. Traveling to the cow's liver, the fluke's life cycle begins again.

BY THE NUMBERS

A liver fluke can live inside a cow for **six months** to **two years.**

CRITTER REPORT

HOW DO LIVER FLUKES LIVE INSIDE A COW'S GUTS?

LIVER FLUKES, *Dicrocoelium dendriticum,* are large **leaf-shaped flatworms** called trematodes. They live inside cows' guts! How do they resist getting smushed around and ground up in an acid bath like the cow's food? The fluke has evolved a **TOUGH OUTER LAYER** of tissue that protects it against the cow's digestive juices. While grass and hay are ground up and dissolved into nutrients, the liver fluke lives on, feeding on the cow's body tissues and blood.

THIS LIVER FLUKE HAS BODY ARMOR TO PROTECT IT FROM BEING DIGESTED.

ATTACK OF THE RODENTS

"HERE, KITTY, KITTY!" The parasite *Toxoplasma gondii* is a tricky little monster. It reproduces inside of cats' stomachs. But how does it get there? First it infects the brains of mice and rats—cats' natural prey! If a cat eats an infected mouse or rat, the parasite can reproduce inside the feline's intestines.

BY THE NUMBERS

Studies show that **30 to 50 percent** of the world's population (about 60 million people in the United States) may be exposed to or **infected** by *T. gondii*.

ZOMBIFICATION

Toxoplasma gondii is naturally found in soil, water, and on plants. Just by sniffing around and eating its usual diet, a mouse can ingest *T. gondii*, which travels to the rodent's brain. The parasites cause thousands of tiny capsules, or cysts, to form inside the brain. The cysts cause permanent structural changes to the brain, altering the mouse's behavior. Within three weeks of infection, the "zombie" mouse loses its fear of cats. What's more, it becomes fatally attracted to the scent of cat urine.

The brainwashed mouse moseys over to the cat's litter box. *Pounce!* When the cat swallows the rodent, *T. gondii* travels to the intestines— the perfect place for it to reproduce. After the cat uses the litter box, the parasites are passed on to the environment in the cat's poop, and the cycle begins again. Cats rarely have symptoms when infected by *T. gondii*, so pet owners wouldn't know if their cat is carrying the parasite.

HORROR OR HELPER?

Some people theorize that *T. gondii* might **ALTER THE BEHAVIOR** of not only rodents but also **people** infected by the parasite. Scientists have been studying a possible link between *T. gondii* infection and some **mental health disorders.** The hope is that if a connection is found, scientists can work on **new treatments** for the disorders.

DID YOU KNOW?

Toxoplasma gondii can also infect humans, but most people never show symptoms. Pregnant women should avoid cleaning the litter box to prevent infection.

FROG FEAST

MEET THE MONSTER

THE PARASITIC FLATWORM *RIBEIROIA ONDATRAE* HAS A "MONSTROUS" WAY OF MANIPULATING ITS HOPPY HOST. It causes deformities in a frog's legs, which make the frog easy prey for hungry birds. The flatworm then reproduces in the bird's gut. It's an "un-hoppy" ending for the frog, but it works wonders for the flatworm.

ZOMBIFICATION

First, the flatworm invades a snail that commonly lives in marshy wetlands in the western United States. Inside the snail, the flatworm clones itself and turns the snail into a "flatworm farm." Each night, the zombified snail releases hundreds of flatworm larvae into the marsh.

Flatworm larvae seek out bullfrog tadpoles and burrow through their skin. Suddenly, the young frogs' bodies are not their own—the larvae seize control and form cysts on the tadpoles' developing limbs. The cysts interfere with the process of metamorphosis from tadpole to frog, and the frogs' legs grow out of control! A zombie bullfrog grows with fewer, extra, or malformed legs. Is it any wonder that the zombie frog has a hard time jumping or swimming? It falls prey to a hungry predator, like a heron. When the bird eats the frog, the flatworm reproduces in the bird's intestines. The bird then poops, releasing flatworm eggs into the water. A snail slurps the eggs, and the zombie process keeps on hopping!

BY THE NUMBERS

In a lab, scientists found that the **jumps** of malformed frogs were **41 percent shorter** than the jumps of healthy frogs. The zombie frogs also swam **37 percent slower**, making them easy snacks for hungry birds.

SAVORY SNAIL

MEET THE MONSTER

ARE YOUR EYES BUG- GING OUT? Don't say we didn't warn you! A microscopic worm, *Leucochloridium paradoxum*, makes the eyes of its host snail wiggle like cater- pillars to attract birds. It's all part of the worm's bizarre reproductive plan.

ZOMBIFICATION

The eye-popping process begins when an amber snail nibbles on bird poo infected with worm eggs. (Hey, a snail's gotta eat!) The worm's eggs develop into sporocysts, whitish tissue that grows like a tumor in the snail's liver. The spooky sporocyst then branches out, taking over the snail's body until it reaches the critter's eyestalks. There it deposits a sac full of worm larvae—gross!

Ready for the zombie dance? The larvae make the eye- stalks bulge with fluid, so the snail can't pull them back in. They start to wiggle and jiggle like caterpillars. There is one catch: Snails are nocturnal (meaning they're active at night). But most birds feed by day. So the worm manipulates its host, forcing it to head out into daylight, where dangers such as hungry predators abound.

A bird notices the pulsating "caterpillars" and snaps them up for a juicy snack. But instead of eating a real caterpillar, the bird ingests a worm-infested meal. The bird's intestines are the perfect spot for the parasites to reproduce. Eventually, the bird poops out the worm's eggs. An unsuspecting snail comes by to taste the infected bird droppings, and here we are again, back at the beginning of the zombie snail tale.

BY THE NUMBERS

Strangely, zombified snails are **three times more active** than healthy snails. A scientist observed a zombie snail moving **three feet** (1 m) in **15 minutes**— that's speedy for a snail!

ZOMBIE APOCALYPSE!

Zombies seem to be invading everywhere you turn—in movies, books, on TV, even on the street (well, on Halloween at least!). Why is there so much zombie zaniness out there?

The term "zombie" comes from voodoo folklore in Haiti and New Orleans, Louisiana, U.S.A., in which a zombie refers to a dead body brought back to life. In the 17th and 18th centuries, Haiti (then called Saint-Domingue) was under French rule. The French enslaved Africans to work on sugar plantations. The work was brutal and sometimes deadly. According to legend, a voodoo god known as Baron Samedi would gather dead slaves from their graves and bring them to a heavenly afterlife in Africa. But if the slaves somehow offended the god, they would be condemned to be undead slaves forever— zombies without a soul.

After the end of French rule in 1804, zombies remained part of Haitian folklore. As part of the voodoo faith, Haitians believed that sorcerers or magicians called bocor had the power to "create" zombies, raise them from the grave, and force them to do their bidding. Some say the bocor turned people into zombies by giving them a potion containing poison from a puffer fish. This would paralyze the victims so that they appeared dead and were buried. A few hours later the bocor unearthed the zombies and forced them into slavery.

Today, zombie myths remain— but most renditions are based more on science than on magic. In American pop culture, zombies come back to life through a wide variety of scientific causes—for example, a viral infection, radiation from a space probe, or mutations of diseases like rabies, mad cow, or measles. These days, a mythical zombie attack is often linked to a global pandemic, the catastrophic spread of a world-wide disease.

Although human zombies remain in movies, scientists continue to be amazed by the real-life zombies they discover in nature and the countless surprising (and often gruesome) ways that creatures take over the brains of other living things to survive.

TODAY, ZOMBIE STORIES ARE STILL POPULAR.

THIS HAITIAN PAINTING DEPICTS A BOCOR AND HIS NEWLY CREATED ZOMBIES.

ZOMBIE EMERGENCY KIT

In 2011, the U.S. Centers for Disease Control and Prevention (CDC) published *Preparedness 101: Zombie Pandemic,* with tips on how to survive a **zombie invasion—or any emergency situation,** such as earthquakes, volcanoes, and floods.

Try creating your own emergency kit with the following items:

WATER & FOOD

STOCK UP ON NON-PERISHABLE ITEMS (SUCH AS CANNED FOOD) AND DRINKING WATER (YOU'LL NEED ONE GALLON [3.8 L] PER PERSON PER DAY).

TOOLS & SUPPLIES

AVOID EMERGENCY SITUATIONS—AND ZOMBIES!—WITH DUCT TAPE, A BATTERY-POWERED RADIO, AND A FLASHLIGHT,

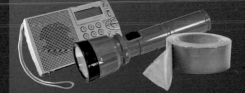

IMPORTANT DOCUMENTS

STORE COPIES OF YOUR PASSPORT AND BIRTH CERTIFICATE.

FIRST AID SUPPLIES

ALTHOUGH YOU'RE A GONER IF A ZOMBIE BITES YOU, YOU CAN USE FIRST AID SUPPLIES TO TREAT BASIC CUTS AND LACERATIONS THAT YOU MIGHT GET DURING A TORNADO OR HURRICANE.

CHAPTER 2

BLOOD-SUCKERS

VICIOUS VAMPIRES

"I want to suck your blood!" Even before Bram Stoker's *Dracula* appeared in 1897, with the title character's sharp fangs, fancy cape, and slick black hair, vampires had been invading people's minds for centuries. The Mesopotamians, ancient Greeks, Chinese, Indians, and Romans all shared spooky myths about bloodsucking spirits. During the Middle Ages in Europe, frightening rumors spread about animated corpses arising from their graves and haunting the living by drinking their blood. Back then, superstitious people searched to blame someone—or something—for the spread of deadly diseases.

These gruesome legends have endured the test of time. Bloodsucking vampires are alive and well in today's pop culture. And they are also alive and well right in the real world! In fact, about 14,000 animal species thrive on blood!

Why do these animal vampires have such a gruesome appetite? For many, a bloody banquet, packed with water and protein, is the difference between life and death. And the liquid is plentiful in nature. This chapter will explore how certain animals feast on blood, and the body structures that make them super suckers.

HUMANS AREN'T THE ONLY VICTIMS. HERE, A MOSQUITO SUCKS THE BLOOD OF A REPTILE.

MUNCHING MOSQUITOES

MEET THE MONSTER

MOSQUITOES ARE ALL ABOUT BUZZ, BITES, AND SUCKING BLOOD. So you might be surprised to learn that male mosquitoes are actually vegetarian. They have a nectar-based diet. But not the egg-laying females! These flying "vampires" get their protein from blood—sometimes from humans.

•••• HORROR OR HELPER? ••••

ITCHY, RED BUMPS may seem tame compared to the curse of becoming a vampire, but in addition to causing annoying welts, some species of mosquitoes may carry **dangerous diseases** such as **malaria, Zika, West Nile, yellow fever,** and **dengue fever.** Mosquito-borne diseases cause **millions of deaths** in developing countries every year. So, does the world actually need mosquitoes? Humans might despise the annoying insects (scientific name Culicidae), but **in nature they are beneficial.** Birds, frogs, lizards, fish, bats, and other animals eat them. Mosquito larvae also eat organic matter in wetlands, recycling nutrients back into the ecosystem.

DID YOU KNOW?

These spiders look scary, but they are "mosquito terminators" ... also known as real-life vampire slayers! They specialize in hunting down malaria-carrying mosquitoes. No wooden stakes needed!

Like mythical vampires, mosquitoes have cunning ways of sneaking up on their prey. From as far away as 100 feet (30 m), mosquitoes can sense carbon dioxide, the gas that we give off when we exhale. The annoying insects also use their antennae to track body odors, and can sense heat and movements. Then they zoom in on their prey. It's slurpin' time!

When a female mosquito lands on a victim, she pierces the skin. Not with fangs like mythical vampires, but with her proboscis: a long, thin, pointy structure that forms a part of her mouth. One tube in the proboscis injects an enzyme, a type of protein that stops blood from clotting and clogging her food tube. The other tube sucks the free-flowing blood into the insect's body. Mosquitoes use blood for nourishment and also as protein for the eggs developing in the bug's abdomen.

Although mythical vampires leave bite marks, mosquitoes leave itchy red welts on humans and animals. These bumps are actually an allergic reaction to the bug's saliva.

How can people stop the pesky beasts? Not with garlic, which kept Dracula away. If you're outside, cover up or use insect repellent. Mosquitoes are also attracted to cologne, perfume, and scented body lotion, and they tend to be drawn to dark clothing—all things to keep in mind when you fear being attacked by a flying mini-vampire!

BY THE NUMBERS
The average mosquito weighs **.000088 ounce** (2.5 mg).

CRITTER REPORT

VAMPIRE-FREE ZONE?

Iceland is a **VAMPIRE-FREE ZONE,** at least when it comes to mosquitoes. The country is one of the **only habitable places on Earth** that doesn't host these aggravating insects. No one is sure why. After all, Iceland isn't nearly as cold as Antarctica, where it's too frigid for mosquitoes (or humans) to survive for long periods. Plus, **Iceland has lots of ponds and lakes,** where mosquitoes thrive. Some scientists say that the **chemical makeup of Iceland's soil** might repel mosquitoes. What's more, **Iceland's climate cycle** of freezing and thawing may also keep the little flying beasts at bay. A **WARMING CLIMATE,** however, may mean that Icelanders could be swatting these bloodsuckers in the future.

VAMPIRE BATS

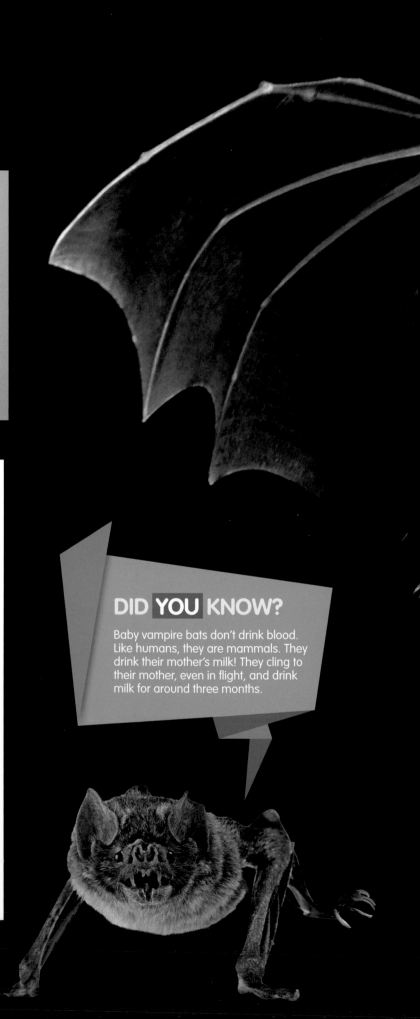

MEET THE MONSTER

WHEN YOU HEAR THE WORD "VAMPIRE," YOU PROBABLY THINK OF BATS—FLITTERING IN THE MOONLIGHT AND READY TO SUCK SOME BLOOD! Vampire bats, which may have helped inspire some of the most popular vampire lore, are the only mammals that feed entirely on blood. Like mythical vampires, they are nocturnal and have sharp fangs that can pierce animal skin. Vampire bats mainly feed on animals, like cattle, but sometimes they drink the blood of humans, too!

BLOODSUCKER BIO

Like their mythical counterparts, vampire bats (scientific name Desmodontinae) have keen senses of sight and smell. Bats have also developed a specialized navigation system known as echolocation. They give off high-pitched sounds that humans can't hear. The sounds travel in waves and bounce off any object—or animal—they come across. The bat listens for the echoes that return: *"Mmm, I hear my juicy dinner calling!"* By calculating how long it takes for the sound to return, a bat can locate its prey. The bat's brain also detects how big the animal is and in which direction it is moving. A bat's echolocation is so exact that it can detect an insect in flight!

When vampire bats attack, a sensor in their nose detects a spot where warm blood is flowing. Then their razor-sharp teeth puncture their prey's skin. Unlike Dracula, they don't suck blood with their fangs. When they open a wound, they dip their long, double-grooved tongue into the blood and flick it back and forth lapping up a liquid meal. The bat's saliva prevents blood from clotting.

Contrary to popular belief, a vampire bat bite isn't fatal; in fact, many victims sleep peacefully through the attack. Although these flying creatures of the night may carry diseases, like rabies, the risk of catching a disease from a bat is very slim and can be avoided by keeping your distance.

DID YOU KNOW?

Baby vampire bats don't drink blood. Like humans, they are mammals. They drink their mother's milk! They cling to their mother, even in flight, and drink milk for around three months.

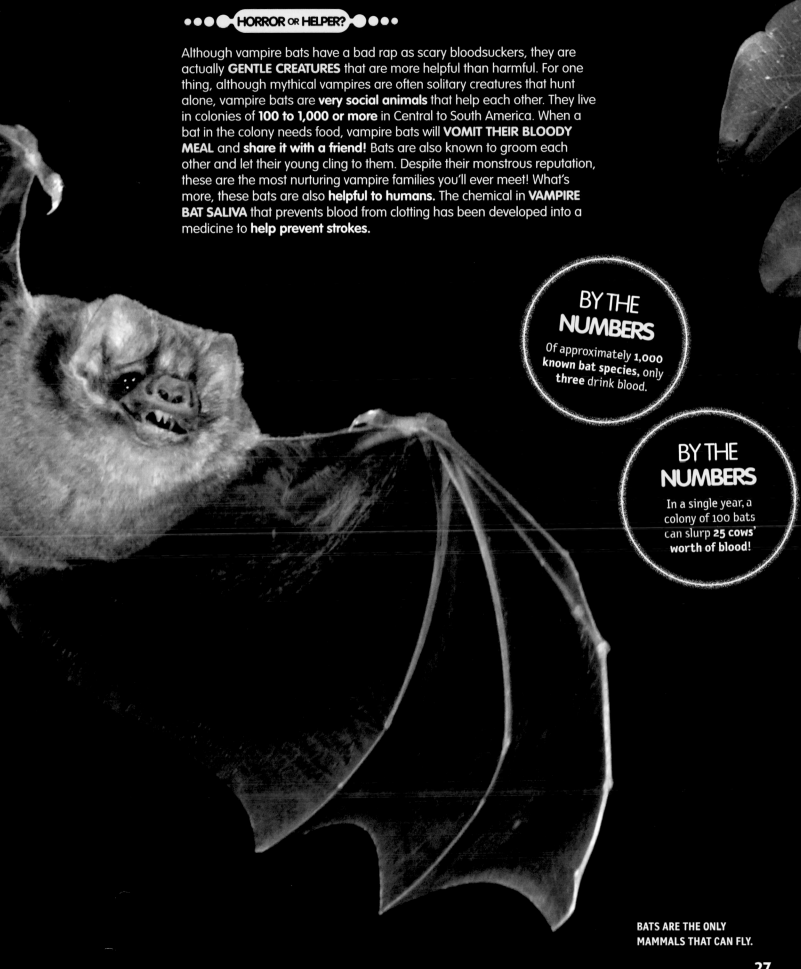

Although vampire bats have a bad rap as scary bloodsuckers, they are actually **GENTLE CREATURES** that are more helpful than harmful. For one thing, although mythical vampires are often solitary creatures that hunt alone, vampire bats are **very social animals** that help each other. They live in colonies of **100 to 1,000 or more** in Central to South America. When a bat in the colony needs food, vampire bats will **VOMIT THEIR BLOODY MEAL** and **share it with a friend!** Bats are also known to groom each other and let their young cling to them. Despite their monstrous reputation, these are the most nurturing vampire families you'll ever meet! What's more, these bats are also **helpful to humans.** The chemical in **VAMPIRE BAT SALIVA** that prevents blood from clotting has been developed into a medicine to **help prevent strokes.**

BY THE NUMBERS
Of approximately **1,000 known bat species,** only **three** drink blood.

BY THE NUMBERS
In a single year, a colony of 100 bats can slurp **25 cows' worth of blood!**

BATS ARE THE ONLY MAMMALS THAT CAN FLY.

BAT MAN
DR. MERLIN TUTTLE

The first time a vampire bat bit Dr. Merlin Tuttle was when Tuttle was in college. He had traveled to Chiapas, Mexico, to help collect bat specimens for the American Museum of Natural History in New York, U.S.A. While Tuttle was removing a bat from a net, the little vampire took a small chunk out of his ungloved finger. "I was bleeding profusely thanks to the anticoagulant [blood thinner] in the bat's saliva," says Tuttle. He soon recovered from his wound—without turning into a vampire!

Tuttle knew that when not defending themselves, the little flying mammals are usually gentle and highly social. Like humans, vampire bats share food and information, adopt orphaned bats, and are caring to other bats that have helped them in the past. Vampire bats are also known to cuddle and greet each other with wing hugs—not exactly vicious behavior!

Tuttle has spent more than 55 years studying bats and debunking myths about them. When he was nine, he discovered a colony of

bats living in an old cabin, and he's been hooked ever since. At 17, he visited a colony of gray bats (*Myotis grisescens*) in a cave near his home in Knoxville, Tennessee, U.S.A. He had read that the bats didn't migrate but instead lived in the same caves year-round. A budding scientist, Tuttle observed this wasn't the case. The gray bats disappeared for the winter and returned in the spring.

Armed with field notes and specimens, Tuttle traveled with his mother to the Smithsonian in Washington, D.C., hoping to meet with a scientist to discuss his theory. Two enthusiastic bat specialists met with Tuttle and encouraged him to set up his first experiment to track the bats using metal bands on their arms.

Eventually, with the help of volunteers, Tuttle tracked 41,000 gray bats across a dozen states! Tuttle proved that gray bats do in fact migrate.

In 1982, Tuttle started an organization called Bat Conservation International to help protect bats around the world, as many populations are shrinking and threatened with extinction. Threats include habitat destruction, overhunting in certain areas where bats are used as food, and the spread of a mysterious disease known as white nose syndrome that has killed millions of bats in North America.

Tuttle's lifelong mission has been to convince people that bats aren't scary, disease-carrying creatures. He's taken thousands of photos showing bats eating nectar, flying, and caring for their pups. His photos show that bats are more helpful than harmful. They eat insect pests, pollinate flowers, and spread seeds. The more people understand bats, he says, the more they care about them.

Here's what Merlin Tuttle and other **bat scientists** need to explore bat caves:

HELMET

PROTECTS FROM THE RAIN OF BAT DROPPINGS (GUANO) AND PEE FROM ABOVE, PLUS BLOODSUCKING INSECTS CALLED BAT MITES

BOOTS & GLOVES

MORE GUANO PROTECTION

FLASHLIGHT

ILLUMINATES PITCH-DARK CAVES

CAMERA

USED TO TAKE PHOTOS FOR RESEARCH, ESTIMATING BAT POPULATIONS OVER TIME, AND SHARING WITH THE PUBLIC

RESPIRATOR

KEEPS BAT SCIENTISTS SAFE FROM BREATHING AMMONIA FUMES FROM BAT DROPPINGS AND FROM BEETLES THAT GIVE OFF THE GAS WHEN THEY FEAST ON GUANO

MERLIN TUTTLE'S ORGANIZATION TEACHES PEOPLE AROUND THE WORLD ABOUT THE CONTRIBUTIONS THAT BATS MAKE. FOR EXAMPLE, THE SAME SUBSTANCE IN VAMPIRE BAT SALIVA THAT MADE BLOOD FLOW FROM TUTTLE'S FINGER IS NOW BEING TESTED TO TREAT PEOPLE WHO HAVE SUFFERED STROKES.

LURKING LAMPREYS

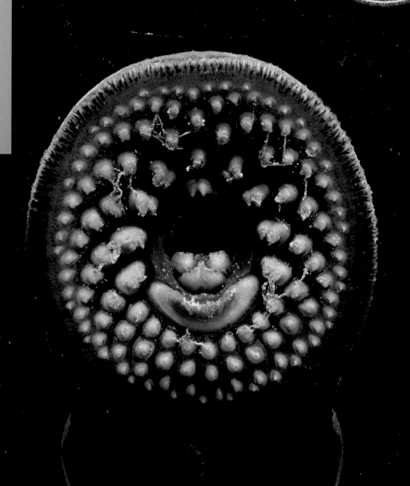

BY THE NUMBERS

A lamprey has **11 or 12 rows of teeth** arranged in circles around its mouth.

MEET THE MONSTER

FROM THE DEEP SHADOWS OF THE WATERY UNDER-WORLD SLITHERS A CREATURE STRAIGHT OUT OF YOUR NIGHTMARES! The sea lamprey is a slimy, eel-shaped fish with no jaws or scales.

BLOODSUCKER BIO

Forget fangs. Instead, a lamprey latches on to a fish host with its suction-cup mouth. Then it digs its hooklike teeth into the victim's flesh and burrows through its scales and body tissue. With its long sharp tongue, the lamprey sucks blood and other body fluids. Like other vampires in nature, lampreys secrete an enzyme to prevent blood from clotting and keep their bloody meal flowing.

In folklore, vampires are thought to be immortal. In a sense, lampreys have achieved a kind of immortality—not as individuals but as a species. They are ancient fish that have been around for more than 340 million years of evolution!

HORROR OR HELPER?

Lampreys hunt in the ocean but migrate to streams to **spawn** (lay eggs). Their young return to the sea. In freshwater streams and rivers in coastal regions (such as the coast of Maine, U.S.A.), lampreys are **IMPORTANT TO THE ECOSYSTEM.** They are food for birds, fish, and mammals, and they help **transport nutrients** from rivers back out to sea.

LUNCHING LEECHES

MEET THE MONSTER

JUST WHEN YOU THOUGHT IT WAS SAFE TO GO BACK IN THE WATER ... you meet these vicious vampires! Leeches are segmented worms, or annelids, and they are notorious bloodsuckers. Most leeches live in freshwater, but some live in oceans or on land. They mostly feed on the blood of fish, amphibians, mammals, and birds—but human blood can provide a delicious snack, too.

BLOODSUCKER BIO

Leeches are double-whammy super suckers—with a small sucker at the mouth end of their body and a large sucker at their rear end. They attach themselves to a host at both ends and suck away!

Some leeches latch on to hosts by using their three sets of jaws—lined with 100 teeth each! They make a Y-shaped cut into the victim's flesh. Their suckers keep them attached to the host. Other "jawless" leeches have a long, pointy proboscis that punctures the flesh of the host.

In some vampire myths, a vampire's bite numbs its prey. *"Don't worry, my pet, this won't hurt a bit!"* A leech's saliva similarly contains an anesthetic, a chemical that numbs the area so the victims don't feel the bite. Leeches also produce other substances to open blood vessels and prevent blood from clotting. A leech can drink 5 to 10 times its weight in blood, swelling like a blimp before falling off its host. Although vampires in folklore had to feed every night, some leeches need to feed only once or twice a year to survive. Now that's something you can sink your teeth into!

•••• HORROR OR HELPER? ••••

Today an **ANTICOAGULANT** that is extracted from European **medicinal leeches** is used to prevent blood clots during surgery. Another chemical from Amazonian leeches dissolves blood clots. Historically, leeches were used by doctors for **BLOODLETTING,** an ancient practice of withdrawing blood from a patient to prevent or treat illness. Today leeches are **making a comeback** in surgery to drain blood and reduce blood clots to prevent stroke and heart disease.

TERRIBLE TICKS

MEET THE MONSTER

THESE TINY ARACHNIDS (ARTHROPODS SUCH AS SPIDERS AND SCORPIONS) CAN DRINK UP TO 600 TIMES THEIR BODY WEIGHT IN BLOOD! But the real danger doesn't come from bloodsucking; it comes from the diseases ticks carry. Ticks travel on hosts like dogs and cats, but they also feed on deer, where they pick up and carry bacteria-causing Lyme disease. When the tick bites its next victim (say, a human), its saliva carries the bacteria into the new host.

BLOODSUCKER BIO

Like tricky vampires, ticks tend to go unnoticed. Young, immature ticks can be smaller than the period at the end of this sentence. Before feeding, adults are about the size of a sesame seed, but they can bulge to the size of a pencil eraser when filled with blood. And like mythical vampires with razor-sharp fingernails, ticks have hooked claws on their eight legs, allowing them to grab on to hosts. Although they don't have traditional fangs, ticks have mouthparts designed to pierce the skin. A harpoon-like structure called a hypostome allows a tick to anchor itself on the victim. The tick also oozes a cement-like substance in its saliva, which glues the tick to skin like Dracula clinging to the walls of his castle.

When ready to mate, adult female ticks attach themselves to a host and then suck blood for more than 24 hours. They lay 2,000 to 18,000 eggs over a lifetime. That's a lot of bloodthirsty babies!

IF YOU FIND A TICK ON YOUR BODY, ASK AN ADULT OR A HEALTH PROFESSIONAL TO REMOVE THE TICK. YOU CAN HELP PREVENT TICK BITES BY WEARING LONG SLEEVES AND PANTS OUTDOORS AND USING INSECT REPELLENT. HAVE AN ADULT CHECK YOU FOR BITES AFTER YOU PLAY OUTSIDE.

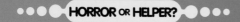

HORROR OR HELPER?

It's not hard to hate bloodsucking ticks, especially because they **SPREAD DISEASE.** But ticks are a primary **source of food** for other animals like birds. They are also hosts to lots of microorganisms like bacteria and viruses, which are **PART OF THE DIVERSITY OF LIFE ON EARTH.** Ticks also help **control populations** of their animal hosts, maintaining a **balance in the ecosystem.**

FIENDISH FLEAS

MEET THE MONSTER

FLEAS ARE TINY WING-LESS INSECTS, BUT THEY CAN HOLD THEIR OWN IN THE "HIGH-STAKES" WORLD OF BLOODSUCKING VAMPIRES. Like Dracula, known for his supernatural ability to leap long distances, a flea's hind legs make it one of the best jumpers in the world relative to its body size. Fleas don't have fangs, but they can still be a pain in the neck! A flea's tubelike mouthparts work like a sharp drinking straw that pierces a victim's skin. They also have keen senses like vampires of lore. In the pupa stage of development, a flea may hang out in its cocoon for up to a year, waiting to sense the body heat or vibrations of a potential host. It can survive for long stretches of time eating next to nothing. However, ravenous young fleas need to feast on blood right away.

BLOODSUCKER BIO

In the Middle Ages, "vampires" were often blamed for the unexplained spread of disease. Superstitious villagers weren't completely wrong ... the culprits were actually *miniature* vampires—not humans! Like ticks, fleas are known to spread diseases in their saliva. In medieval times, fleas spread bubonic plague from rats to humans. After biting infected rats, the fleas passed the bacteria *Yersinia pestis* on to humans. The "Black Death," so called because it produced black sores on skin, killed 20 million people in Europe—almost a third of the continent's population—possibly the worst "vampire" invasion of all time!

DID YOU KNOW?

Fleas have body armor! Hard plates called sclerites protect them from getting squashed.

VAMPIRES THROUGH THE AGES

STRIGOI

The world's most popular vampire emerged from the crypt in 1897 in Bram Stoker's classic novel *Dracula*. Since then, vampires have had a "fangtastic" run in movies, TV shows, cartoons, books, and even in the costume aisle.

But Dracula wasn't the first night demon to invade people's imaginations. Legends about evil bloodsucking spirits have haunted cultures around the world for thousands of years. Check out these gruesome characters:

- First mentioned in a Sumerian poem from around 2000 B.C., Lilith was believed to be an ancient demon from Babylonian culture who lived on the blood of babies.
- Over 2,000 years ago, the ancient Greeks believed in the goddess Empusa, who transformed into a young woman and sucked the blood of men as they slept.
- Stories of *jiang shi*, vampiric ghouls, first appeared in ancient China during the Qing dynasty (1644–1912).
- In the 12th century, one Romanian ghoul, a two-hearted corpse known as Strigoi, was said to drink milk as his beverage of choice. But when it ran out, he sucked blood!

Over time, gory tales of vampires crept into large European cities. In one Serbian village, rumors spread of a vampire invasion!

Why did this "vampire mania" spread? One theory: Massive numbers of people were dying from unknown causes in epidemics like the Black Death. Because people lived in cramped, filthy homes with no sanitation, diseases spread easily. No one understood that bacteria and viruses cause diseases, and these unknown sicknesses often had no cure. Villagers would look for someone—or

something—to blame. Often they would accuse someone who had recently died as being a vampire and the source of the deaths. They would dig up his grave and drive a stake through his heart—thinking that would end the epidemic.

Centuries later, Bram Stoker, who was well versed in vampire mythology, created Dracula. This infamous demon was based on a real-life Romanian ruler from the 1400s notoriously named Vlad the Impaler. Vlad was known for impaling (or stabbing) his enemies with stakes. Stoker also invented new mythology for Dracula, such as his ability to transform into a bat and the notion that his reflection didn't appear in mirrors.

Today's fictional vampires have many of the classic vampire traits—characteristics also shared by many "vampires" in nature—like bloodsucking fangs, incredible strength, leaping, flying, and sleeping by day to hunt at night. The creators of vampires in today's pop culture add new bloodcurdling thrills and chills all the time!

VLAD III WAS THE REAL-LIFE INSPIRATION BEHIND DRACULA.

THE ACTOR BELA LUGOSI
STARS AS DRACULA IN
THE CLASSIC 1931 FILM.

CHAPTER 3

CREEPS FROM THE DEEP

SINISTER SEA MONSTERS

Oceans can be chilly, dark, and mysterious places ... the perfect spots for monsters to manifest! Throughout the ages, sailors have reported eyewitness accounts of sea monsters and other fantastical beasts that lie beneath the waves. You may have heard tales about the legendary leviathan, the giant squidlike kraken, massive sea serpents, or Godzilla emerging from the surf. The mind can play tricks on a sleepy sailor, keeping watch late at night, thousands of miles from shore. But maybe seeing is believing!

In recent years, ocean explorers have had close encounters with some real-life "sea monsters." All of these creatures have developed unique traits that enable them to thrive in the challenging ocean environment. Some have evolved to be perfect predators. Others use ingenious techniques to find mates and to lure and capture prey. Many are amazing masters of disguise. Whichever it is, these watery beasts are sure to give you "creeps from the deep"!

A PEACOCK MANTIS SHRIMP WATCHES OVER ITS EGGS.

PERILOUS PORTUGUESE MAN-OF-WAR

MEET THE MONSTER

THIS CREATURE MIGHT LOOK LIKE A HARMLESS BALLOON, BUT YOU WOULDN'T WANT IT AT YOUR BIRTHDAY PARTY ... it's an inflatable bubble of terror! The Portuguese man-of-war, *Physalia physalis*, is actually not a single animal (like a jellyfish), but a colony of organisms working together as one. Scientists call this type of creature a siphonophore.

CREEP FROM THE DEEP

Attached to the bubble and trailing beneath the waves are dozens of tentacles, which can extend up to 165 feet (50 m) long. These tentacles might seem meant to drag you down to the watery depths, but they are actually covered with venom-packed cells called nematocysts. Once the venom does its work, the tentacles draw prey to the jelly's digestive organs.

Though frightening, the Portuguese man-of-war doesn't swim on its own. Its balloon sail allows it to drift on ocean currents or get blown across the water's surface by winds. Few predators dare to come close, but there are exceptions. Loggerhead sea turtles, which have skin too thick to feel a sting (even on their tongue and throat), chow down on man-of-wars. The blue sea slug also dines on the purple bubbles and stores the stinging nematocysts in its own tissues for defense. Another species, the blanket octopus, is immune to man-of-war stings. It tears off man-of-war tentacles and uses them as weapons! It's a "monster-eat-monster" world!

BY THE NUMBERS

Sometimes armies of man-of-wars float together in squadrons of **1,000 or more!**

38

KILLER CONE SNAIL

BY THE NUMBERS

The geographic cone snail wins the crown as the **most venomous** of 500 known cone snail species. Its venom is a mixture of **hundreds of different toxins.**

MEET THE MONSTER

THIS SEA MONSTER MIGHT SEEM LIKE A GOVERNMENT EXPERIMENT GONE WRONG OR A DEEP-SEA ASSASSIN. The geographic cone snail, *Conus geographus,* which lives in Indo-Pacific reefs, has a secret weapon—it shoots venom through its nose! The cone snail is armed with a potion of nerve toxins that it shoots through a radula tooth, a harpoon-like structure at the end of its proboscis.

CREEP FROM THE DEEP

Because the snail is slow moving, the harpoon is a quick way of capturing fish, marine worms, mollusks, and other prey before they can escape. The toxins paralyze prey instantly. The cone snail then pulls back the radula like a fishing line, drawing its prey into its mouth. It swallows its prey whole.

The cone snail spits out undigested parts of its delicious dinner, like scales and spines, plus the used radula. But each time the cone snail fires a new venom-packed radula, it must reload before firing again. The snail keeps about 20 radulae handy, which its body produces in-house.

One sting from a cone snail has enough venom to kill 15 people. Its venom has caused at least 30 known human deaths. The stings usually occur when deep-sea divers handle the bright-colored snails. There is no known cure. The best advice: Don't touch these snails of doom!

●●●●● **HORROR** OR **HELPER?** ●●●●●

Drug companies are researching cone snails' toxins for possible use in **PAINKILLERS** and a **treatment** for **epilepsy, Alzheimer's, Parkinson's,** and other diseases.

SEA SERPENT

MEET THE MONSTER

IMAGINE A PREHISTORIC MONSTER LURKING OUT OF SIGHT—ITS TERRIBLE JAWS GAPING, ITS SERPENTLIKE BODY WRITHING. Well, imagine no more: The frilled shark is sometimes called a living fossil. These sea monsters have thrived for 80 million years, though some paleontologists (scientists who study fossils) think they are related to sharks that existed 300 million years ago.

BY THE NUMBERS

Shark attacks are much more rare than you think. What are the odds?

Odds of getting struck by lightning in your lifetime: 1 in 3,000

Odds of being injured by a toilet this year: 1 in 10,000

Odds of getting killed by a shark: 1 in 3.7 million

CREEP FROM THE DEEP

Although no one has seen a frilled shark hunt, scientists theorize that it attacks with a sudden strike, like a snake. In fact, its scientific name is *Chlamydoselachus anguineus,* meaning "snakelike." Researchers also think it may close its frilled gills to create a vacuum that sucks prey into its gaping mouth. Its flexible jaws open extra wide. Like a python, the frilled shark can swallow its prey whole, including fish, squid, and other sharks. Its 300 teeth, with multiple spikes arranged in 25 rows, are pointed like arrows toward the creature's throat. *"This way to my stomach!"* The chance of escape is next to zero. The shark's bright white teeth may also act like a lure in the dark, attracting prey to their ultimate doom.

Frilled sharks are known to live around the world, though most specimens have been found off the coast of Japan. They are sometimes caught in deep trawling fishing nets, but humans almost never see them alive. They rarely swim to the surface, and they do not survive for long outside their cold, dark environment. Let's hope they stay outta sight!

●●●●◖ HORROR ᴏʀ HELPER? ◗●●●●

As **CARNIVOROUS** (meat-eating) **apex predators,** sharks swim at the top of the ocean food chain. Their sharp teeth and keen instincts have made them the villains in many horror stories and movies. Despite their chilling reputation, sharks are much **more likely to be killed by humans** than the other way around. **OVERFISHING** has caused a sharp decline in shark populations. Fishermen kill as many as **100 million sharks each year** for their fins, which are used in an expensive soup that is popular in Asia. Sharks have a hard time bouncing back because **they take years to mature** and they **produce few young.** More efforts are needed to protect these misunderstood mammoths of the sea.

DID YOU KNOW?

A female frilled shark may be pregnant for up to three and a half years, nearly twice as long as an African elephant. Baby frilled sharks emerge from eggs inside their mothers and feed on the eggs' yolk until they are born. Between 2 and 15 pups are born at a time.

FRILLED SHARKS SPORT OVERSIZE MOUTHS, EXTRA GILLS WITH A BLOOD-RED TINGE, AND A LONG, THIN BODY THAT MAY HAVE INSPIRED SEA SERPENT MYTHS. THEY MOVE LIKE 6.5-FOOT (2-M)-LONG EELS, SLITHERING THROUGH THE DEEP SEA AS FAR DOWN AS 5,200 FEET (1,585 M).

SHARK SCIENTIST
JESSICA CRAMP

JESSICA CRAMP SPEAKS ABOUT SHARKS AT NATIONAL GEOGRAPHIC IN WASHINGTON, D.C.

Jessica Cramp grew up in the mountains of Pennsylvania, U.S.A., more than two hours from the ocean. Sharks weren't even on her radar. "I wanted to be a fighter pilot, an orthopedic surgeon, or a professional baseball player," she recalls.

But when her dad gave her a set of books called *The Ocean World of Jacques Cousteau*, she was hooked! "I used to dream about being an explorer for National Geographic," she says. "I felt a calling to the ocean."

When Cramp joined a mission to sail across the Pacific Ocean doing research on floating plastic trash, she experienced her first close encounter with sharks. She was paddling on a surfboard with a friend, when someone from the sailboat shouted, "Hey, Jess! Look down!"

"I put my mask on and popped my head underwater. Five gray reef sharks were circling us and following us very curiously!" she recalls. The six-foot (2-m)-long beasts were so close she could see their yellow eyeballs. "I was riveted, but not terrified," Cramp says. "The sharks were just cruising and checking us out."

By the time the sailing crew reached the Cook Islands, Cramp knew she was there to stay. She plunged into marine conservation and began developing a shark sanctuary with one of the locals. Today she is living her dream as a National Geographic Emerging Explorer, pursuing a Ph.D. in shark research and working to protect sharks, which are threatened around the world.

Cramp's research involves tagging sharks and following their movements. She also films them by lowering video cameras into the water. "Most of my work is done on a boat," not swimming with sharks, she says, though she does dive in every once in a while. "I wear a wet suit and gloves. Shark skin feels like sandpaper. It's not often they get close, but if they bump you, your arms can get chafed."

Although we sometimes think of sharks as "monsters," in reality, humans are a much bigger threat to sharks than the other way around. A recent report estimated that humans kill 100 million sharks each year. By contrast, sharks kill about five people worldwide on average.

The biggest threat to sharks is overfishing, Cramp says. Sharks' fins are used in a popular Asian soup. Their liver oil, called squalene, is used in cosmetics.

Many sharks are caught accidentally as "bycatch" in fishing nets. "Because sharks live long, are late to mature, and have very few offspring, they can't replenish as fast as [fishermen] are taking them out of sea," she explains. Other threats include the destruction of coral reefs, which are feeding grounds for sharks, and ocean pollution.

"Sharks are at the top of the ocean food chain. They keep fish populations in check and keep ecosystems in balance," says Cramp. "They've been around for 400 million years. It's important that we don't wipe out the ocean's top predators."

JESSICA CRAMP'S FAVORITE SHARK IS THE HAMMERHEAD. "THEY'RE SO STRANGE-LOOKING!" SHE SAYS. SHE LOVES SHARKS BECAUSE THEY ARE SMART, SLEEK, FAST, AND HAVE INCREDIBLE DIVERSITY.

INTERESTED IN
SHARK RESEARCH?

Things you need to know
before you sign on!

1 "WE SMELL LIKE FISH ALL DAY LONG!" SAYS
CRAMP. "WE SPEND HOURS CHOPPING BAIT
TO DRAW SHARKS TO OUR BOAT."

2 MANY JOBS ARE LINKED TO SHARK
RESEARCH AND MARINE CONSERVATION.
"YOU CAN BE A BIOLOGIST, AN ENGINEER, AN
ECONOMIST, LAWYER, TEACHER, OR BOAT
DRIVER," SAYS CRAMP.

3 TO BE A SHARK SCIENTIST, CRAMP SAYS,
"YOU NEED TO BE COMFORTABLE IN THE
WATER AND ON BOATS, BE ABLE TO THINK ON
YOUR FEET, BE REALLY GOOD AT SCIENCE, AND
BE VERY DETAIL ORIENTED."

4 "YOU NEED TO HAVE A PASSION FOR WHAT
YOU DO AND BE ABLE TO LEARN AND GAIN
SKILLS AS YOU GO ALONG," CRAMP ADDS.

5 MOST OF ALL, YOU CAN'T HAVE
GALEOPHOBIA ... A FEAR OF SHARKS!

CRAMP ALSO WORKS TO
HELP PRESERVE AND
PROTECT THE OCEAN.

DIVING IN THE
GALÁPAGOS ISLANDS,
CRAMP IS NOT AFRAID
OF SHARKS.

SPINE-CHILLING STINGER

MEET THE MONSTER

THEY'RE AS SMALL AS YOUR THUMBNAIL, BUT DON'T LET THAT FOOL YOU. The Irukandji, a species of box jellyfish, is one of the most venomous creatures in the world. Once this jellyfish stings, the symptoms can be excruciating—back pain, vomiting, muscle cramps, and in extremely rare cases, death. Some people who are stung experience an eerie symptom: an overwhelming feeling of doom.

CREEP FROM THE DEEP

Like the Portuguese man-of-wars, the jellyfish deliver their poison via nematocysts (tiny stinging capsules). Divers often wear protective suits in areas where Irukandji have been spotted, like the reefs off Queensland, Australia. Don't worry too much, though—some sources say that only three people worldwide have died from Irukandji stings in the past 100 years.

Unlike other species of jellyfish, the Irukandji have stingers not only on their tentacles but also on their bell. Despite their size, their sting is 100 times as venomous as a cobra's and 1,000 times stronger than a tarantula's bite. That's one mighty mini-monster!

DID YOU KNOW?

A group of jellyfish is called a smack, bloom, or swarm.

HORROR OR HELPER?

Compounds in box **JELLYFISH VENOM** have been used to treat **cancer** and **arthritis**.

SHOCKING SHRIMP

MEET THE MONSTER

SOMETIMES THE SCARIEST MONSTERS ARE THE ONES YOU LEAST SUSPECT! This tiny crustacean's rainbow of colors might seem attractive, but when the peacock mantis shrimp, *Odontodactylus scyllarus*, takes a swing at its prey with its clublike limbs, look out! The shrimp's punch is powerful enough to crack the shell of a crab, snail, or clam (otherwise known as lunch). The force also makes the surrounding water boil, maiming the prey.

BY THE NUMBERS

More powerful than a professional boxer's wallop, the punch of a peacock mantis shrimp can strike with the speed of a .22-caliber bullet— 50 times faster than the blink of an eye.

CREEP FROM THE DEEP

Think you can sneak away? This little guy has its eyes on you— in fact, it can see 10 times more color than a human can see, including ultraviolet light. Plus, each eye moves independently. One eye can look left while the other looks right. Talk about creeps of the deep!

Some people think that peacock mantis shrimp would make beautiful additions to a fish tank. Two problems: (1) The shrimp have a voracious appetite and may eat the other creatures in the tank, and (2) they can break through the aquarium's glass with their powerful punch!

HORROR OR HELPER?

Scientists are studying the peacock mantis shrimp's **UNIQUE VISION** to help improve CDs, DVDs, Blu-ray, and **holographic technology**.

45

GIANT JELLY

MEET THE MONSTER

AS FAR AS GIANTS GO, GODZILLA HAS MET HIS MATCH! With a bell stretching up to eight feet (more than 2.4 m) wide, this monstrous beast is the world's largest jellyfish. It lurks in the chilly seas of the Arctic, northern Pacific, and Atlantic Oceans. Known as the lion's mane, it gets its name from its shaggy, reddish yellow "mane" of 800 to 1,200 stinging tentacles. They can trail as long as 100 feet (30 m). That's longer than a blue whale, one of the world's longest animals!

CREEP FROM THE DEEP

Each tentacle is lined with a nasty, stinging nematocyst (small cell). When the cell is triggered by hair coming into contact with a victim, it fires a tiny "harpoon" that injects venom. The paralyzed prey—which may include other jellies, small fish, shrimp, and crustaceans—becomes an easy victim, and the jellyfish, *Cyanea capillata,* draws its helpless prey into its mouth using four thick, frilled "oral arms."

But here's something truly gross: The jellyfish's mouth also serves as its rear end. After food passes through the jellyfish's mouth, it enters a space that serves as a gullet (a passageway for food), stomach, and intestine all in one. Once the prey is digested, waste products exit through the same hole that they originally entered ... meaning the jellyfish eats and poops through the same hole!

What's more, jellyfish pack the ultimate monster weapon: They can keep on stinging even after they are dead. On June 16, 2010, the remains of a single lion's mane jellyfish stung around 100 swimmers in New Hampshire, U.S.A., after officials tried to remove it from the beach. Even though the jellyfish was dead, the surf was loaded with thousands of venomous, stinging tentacles. The stings were painful, but not deadly. Ready to go back into the water, anyone?

●●●○ HORROR OR HELPER? ○●●●

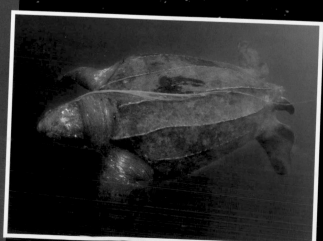

One species' enemy is another species' lunch. **LEATHERBACK SEA TURTLES,** a **critically endangered species,** get their energy from a surprising source: **They eat small lion's mane jellyfish** by the dozens! The turtles capture the jellies in their sharp lips. **Pointed spines** in the turtles' mouth and throat keep the jellyfish from escaping.

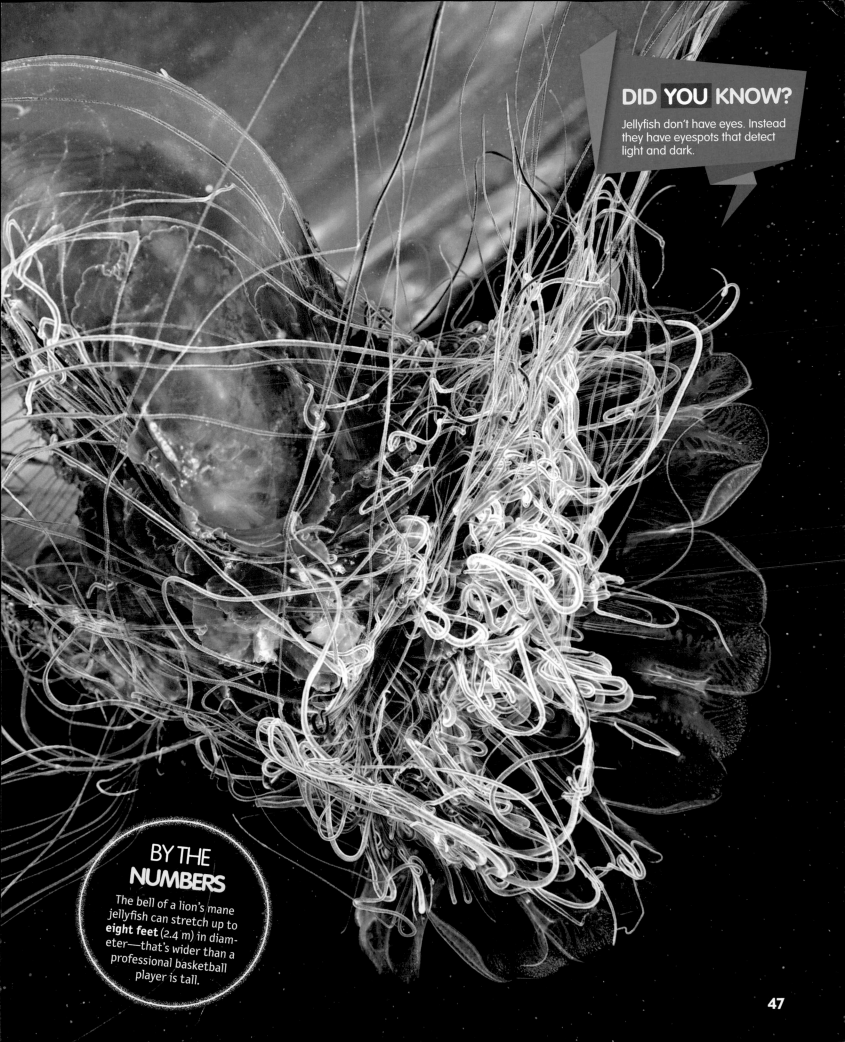

BY THE NUMBERS

The bell of a lion's mane jellyfish can stretch up to **eight feet** (2.4 m) in diameter—that's wider than a professional basketball player is tall.

SUPER SQUID

MEET THE MONSTER

IF YOU THOUGHT MARINE GIANTS WERE JUST A MYTH, THINK AGAIN. These monsters of the deep can grow longer than a school bus! Males can stretch to 33 feet (10 m) long, while the females tend to outsize the males at a whopping 43 feet (13 m). Giant squid *(Architeuthis)* are cephalopods, mollusks whose legs are attached to their head.

DID YOU KNOW?

In two years, a giant squid grows from only an inch (2.5 cm) long at birth to about 20 feet (6 m) long!

CREEP FROM THE DEEP

The giant squid is truly a top predator: Its eight massive, snakelike arms and two long tentacles snag prey, including fish, other squid, and even small whales! Rows of hundreds of suction cups line the arms and tentacles and allow the squid to hold on to its victim. Tiny sharp teeth in the suckers cut into the prey like round saw blades. The limbs draw the meal into the monster's beaklike mouth, which is made of chitin, the same hard material in lobster and crab shells. It resembles the beak of a parrot. Inside the beak is the squid's terrifying tongue, a muscle called a radula. It's lined with rows of razor-sharp hooks that slash the doomed prey to death. Who says sea "monsters" aren't real?

BLUE-RINGED OCTOPUS

RESEARCHERS WERE ABLE TO PHOTOGRAPH THIS GIANT SQUID BY LURING IT WITH BAIT.

CRITTER REPORT
CURIOUS COLORS

Some cephalopods have **DIFFERENT-COLORED CELLS** that make them look **iridescent,** with shimmery blue, green, silver, and gold markings. The **venomous blue-ringed octopus** uses this strategy to produce shiny blue circles to **warn predators of danger:** *"Don't get too close! I have a deadly bite!"* Other cephalopods have cells that **MIRROR THE COLORS OF THEIR ENVIRONMENT** so they blend in. Some octopuses can even change the **texture of their skin** to match nearby rocks and coral. They do this by **controlling bumps** on their skin called **papillae.** The cephalopods change their skin colors and textures based on visual cues in their environment. Their disguise can occur in **less than a second!**

HORROR OR HELPER?

Do giant squid **make you nervous?** The squid's nervous system may actually be helpful to humans. Giant squid have the **LONGEST NERVES** in the animal kingdom. Because the nerves can be **seen without a microscope,** scientists are studying them to better understand how **signals travel** from the brain to other body parts.

YUCKY YETI

MEET THE MONSTER

THE LAST PLACE YOU'D EXPECT TO FIND A SCARY HAIRY CREATURE IS IN THE DEEP SEA. Yet in 2005, scientists studying the chilly depths off Easter Island discovered a hairy-armed creature they named the "yeti crab" for the giant, lumbering yetis of Himalayan folklore. The six-inch (15-cm)-long crustacean is in no way as large as its namesake. Yet instead of living in the frozen tundra like those abominable snowmen, the yeti crab dwells on the edge of steaming hydrothermal vents—cracks in Earth's crust where ocean water is heated by boiling hot magma (liquefied rock).

BY THE NUMBERS

The water around hydro-thermal vents heats up to 750°F (400°C). Talk about a hot meal.

DID YOU KNOW?

Hydrothermal vents form where Earth's tectonic plates spread apart and hot magma wells up. The water is packed with minerals that feed yeti crabs and other deep-sea creatures.

CREEP FROM THE DEEP

Like the mythical yeti, the crab sports furry arms with silky hair. Its scientific name is *Kiwa hirsuta*, because Kiwa was the Polynesian goddess of shellfish and *hirsute* means "hairy"! Yeti crabs hypnotically wave their arms over the hot plumes of water gushing from the vents some 7,200 feet (2,200 m) below the ocean's surface. Scientists think that the yeti crabs are catching bacteria that thrive in the vents. They grow in colonies in the yeti's arm hairs and may provide the crab with a food source! Because the crab is thought to be blind, having a built-in bacterial buffet is a big advantage in the deep sea.

"BLACK SMOKER" VENTS SPEW MINERAL-RICH WATER THAT ALLOWS SEA CREATURES TO THRIVE IN THIS EXTREME ENVIRONMENT.

SNARE OF THE SQUID

MEET THE MONSTER

THE VAMPIRE SQUID LURKS IN TOTAL DARKNESS, WAITING FOR ITS HAPLESS PREY. To adjust to the lack of light in the deep sea, these squid have the largest eyes for their size of any animal on the planet. The squid, *Vampyroteuthis infernalis,* is only about eight inches (20 cm) long, but its marble blue eyes are the size of a wolf's.

CREEP FROM THE DEEP

These squid get their notorious name from their blood-red color and long webbed arms, which resemble a cape. Despite this name, vampire squid don't suck blood. But they do have unique ways of luring and capturing meals. Each of the squid's eight skinny arms has a light-producing organ at the tip that shines bright blue to attract prey. The underside of each arm is lined with suckers near the tips and rows of spiky projections leading up to the mouth. The squid captures its victims by surrounding them in the webbing around its arms. Once they are trapped inside this webbed cage, the spikes push the helpless prey into the squid's mouth.

The squid itself is also a master of defense. When startled, it draws the cape over the rest of its body, with its prickly lining facing inside out. This is described as a "pineapple posture" because it makes the squid look like a spiky fruit instead of a delicious fishy meal.

DID YOU KNOW?

Vampire squid are about the size, shape, and color of a football (with a fin at the end).

GRUESOME GOBLIN
SHARK

MEET THE MONSTER

GOBLINS IN THE SEA? You bet! These deep-sea sharks are the sole survivors of a family called Mitsukurinidae that dates back 125 million years. Despite their gruesome appearance, goblin sharks may seem rather meek. They have a flabby body and small fins, which make them slow swimmers (this helps conserve energy in the chilly depths).

BY THE NUMBERS

Goblin sharks can grow up to 12 feet (4 m) long and weigh up to 460 pounds (209 kg).

DID YOU KNOW?

The Japanese were the first to call the species a goblin shark (*tengu-zame* in Japanese) after a mythical goblin that had a pointed nose.

CREEP FROM THE DEEP

What happens when this slowpoke is on the hunt and a delicious squid swishes out of reach? The shark pops its jaws out of its mouth like a grabbing tool to trap its prey! The jaws are connected to elastic flaps of skin that unfold from its snout like an unfurling sock puppet. The quick motion most likely creates a vacuum to suck prey into the jutting jaws. Goblin sharks gobble down squid, rattail fish, dragonfish, and crustaceans. Then they pull their jaws back into their mouth.

Because the shark has eyes too small to see much in the dark, the underside of its snout is dotted with sensors that detect the electric current given off by other living creatures. The goblin shark also waves its snout over the seabed like a metal detector searching for treasure. For prey, there is little chance of escape. Now that's jaw-dropping!

ALLURING ANGLERFISH

MEET THE MONSTER

IN THE FORBIDDING DEPTHS OF THE OCEAN, MORE THAN 200 SPECIES OF ANGLERFISH ARE ON THE PROWL. Total darkness cloaks their bulbous heads, protruding jaws, and needle-sharp translucent teeth. How do they attract mates and meals?

CREEP FROM THE DEEP

When it comes to keeping away monsters, flicking on a night light usually does the trick. But in the case of the female ceratioid anglerfish, Ceratiidae, a bioluminescent lure, lit up by the light-producing chemical reactions of millions of bacteria, *attracts* a monstrous mate. In the deep, dark sea—about a mile (1.6 km) beneath the surface—the male anglerfish's well-developed eyes spot the female's glowing lure that dangles like a fishing rod hanging between her eyes. The lure's flickering light patterns, shape, and color tell the male when he's spotted a mate. His large nostrils also pick up her alluring scent.

Once he finds her, he won't let go. The male clamps his jaws on to the female's belly and sucks nourishment from her bloodstream. His body releases an enzyme that dissolves the female's skin around the bite. Eventually the skin of the male and female grow together as one. Their blood vessels join so that the female's blood flows through the male's body. His fins and eyes—organs he no longer needs to navigate in the deep—wither away. The two become an inseparable pair, with the male hanging around just to fertilize the female's eggs. Talk about locking in a mate for life!

The female must now hunt for two. Luckily, her lure also attracts prey. When a hapless squid spots the light and swims over to check it out— *snap!* The female extends her giant jaws and chomps her prey with jagged sharp teeth. Lunch is served!

DID YOU KNOW?

A female ceratioid anglerfish can carry about six males attached to her body.

A FEMALE CERATIOID ANGLERFISH WITH A MALE ATTACHED

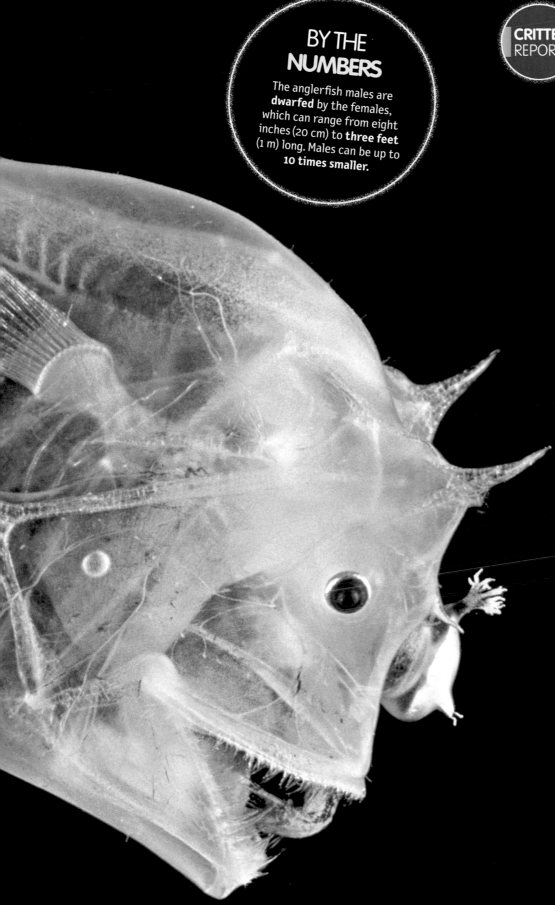

CRITTER REPORT

DEEP-SEA SURVIVAL TACTICS

Crushing pressure. Total darkness. Frigid cold. Little food. **How do creeps of the deep survive** under these monstrous conditions? Over **millions of years,** they have developed many **ADAPTATIONS** to thrive in this harsh environment:

GO WITH THE GLOW: Many deep-sea creatures have the ability to produce light with chemical reactions in their cells (sometimes with the help of bacteria). This feature is called bioluminescence. Creating flashes of light allows deep-sea fish to attract prey—as well as mates—in the dark. Viperfish and anglerfish are flashy examples.

WHAT'S THAT SMELL?: Fishermen who have caught giant squid report a stench. The giant squid produces smelly ammonia gas as a waste product. Ammonia is lighter than seawater. If the squid wants to rise to the surface, it holds in the ammonia. To plunge into the depths, the squid lets the ammonia loose, giving off a potent smell.

BIG MOUTH: A gulper eel has a mouth bigger than the rest of its body. Its mouth becomes unhinged, allowing it to swallow prey larger than itself. That comes in handy when meals are scarce.

OVERSIZE EYES: Many deep-sea creatures, like giant squid and the deep-sea hatchetfish, have oversize eyes to let in the maximum amount of light.

TURN UP THE HEAT: Many deep-sea creatures hang out near hydrothermal vents, underwater hot springs that give off minerals from Earth's crust. In the chilly depths, these plumes heated by magma provide warmth and food for many creatures, including giant tube worms.

CRACKING THE KRAKEN

In the 1700s, a Danish-Norwegian writer named Erik Pontoppidan interviewed sailors who had reported seeing a huge sea monster. The sailors claimed that a creature with giant eyeballs and a beaklike mouth attacked their ship with massive, slithery, sucker-lined tentacles, threatening to pull their entire crew down into the abyss. Pontoppidan named the beast "kraken" and exaggerated its size to be the width of an island. The name "kraken," referring to a sea monster, stuck for nearly 200 years.

By the late 1800s, science began to trump superstition. No one had ever studied a real kraken, dead or alive. Yet long tentacles and strange beaks were discovered in the bellies of dead whales. The whales also had circular scars on their skin, suggesting a battle with a large sea creature with suckers.

Beginning in 1870, the bodies of eight-legged sea creatures with long tentacles mysteriously began to wash up on shores around the world. No one knew why this was occurring. But scientists had evidence of a newly discovered species; they named it *Architeuthis dux*, aka the giant squid. After 10 years, the sightings stopped.

In the 1960s, an American marine biologist named Frederick Aldrich researched the mysterious surfacing of giant squid. He theorized that seasonal cold-water currents whisked the giant squid from icy depths and swept them close to shore. He predicted that the current would return—with the squid—in the 1960s. And he was right! Huge specimens washed up all around the globe, a boon for researchers.

Still, it wasn't until 2004 that scientists from Japan were able to snap photographs of a live giant squid at a depth of more than half a mile (0.8 km). In 2007, fishermen in the Antarctic caught the world's largest specimen, a colossal squid (a cousin of the giant squid), in their fishing nets. Only recently have scientists begun to crack open the mysteries of the real kraken and discover how it lives in the deep dark sea.

MERMAIDS HAVE BEEN POPULAR FOR CENTURIES, AS SEEN IN THIS 1911 DRAWING OF PETER PAN.

MEDIEVAL DRAWING OF A GIANT SEA CREATURE ATTACKING A SAILING SHIP

DEPICTION OF THE
LEGENDARY KRAKEN

CHAPTER 4

ANIMAL ALIENS

ICKY INVADERS

Humans have been captivated by alien invasions since they gazed at the heavens and pondered the existence of life on other planets thousands of years ago. In the 1960s, the belief in aliens sky-rocketed with the success of the U.S. space program. If humans could travel to the moon, why couldn't aliens from other planets land here? Alien movies featuring giant-eyed creatures with oversize heads took off! So did reports of UFO sightings. Even today, UFO reports have risen nationwide, more than tripling since 2001.

So what's the verdict—are aliens really out there? Or ... are they already here? This might give you nightmares, but you are not alone—not now, not ever! Your home and body are hosts to an entire world of microscopic invaders—bacteria, viruses, fungi, even other animals. *"We come in peace (well, some of us, anyway). Resistance is futile."*

Get ready for some close encounters of the microbe kind!

THESE EARWIGS GOT THEIR NAME FROM AN OLD MYTH THAT THEY WOULD ENTER PEOPLE'S EARS, BURROW IN THE BRAIN, AND LAY EGGS!

BODY INVADERS

MEET THE MONSTERS

WHILE YOU GO ABOUT YOUR DAY, TINY BUGS ARE LAYING EGGS, FEEDING ON YOUR DEAD SKIN CELLS, MULTIPLYING, AND CRAWLING ALL OVER YOUR BODY—INSIDE AND OUT! Some of these hitchhikers are mites, tiny arachnids with short, stumpy legs and claws that hold on to your skin for dear life. They hide out in your eyelashes, hair follicles, or cracks and crevices all over your body.

ALIEN ARRIVAL

Humans aren't born with mites, but we acquire them over our lifetime just by being in contact with other humans. By age 20, a quarter of people walk around with mites on board. By age 90, everybody has them!

Why do creepy critters move in, and what can (or should) you do about them? Zoom in on the good, bad, and icky microbes that call your personal spaces home.

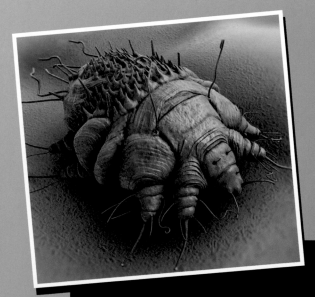

Itch Mite: These arachnids, *Sarcoptes scabiei*, burrow in skin, mostly between fingers, and on wrists, ankles, elbows, buttocks, abdomen, and groin. Skin-melting enzymes enable these critters to burrow under the top layer of skin. They cause a nasty rash; prescription medication is needed.

Demodex brevis: This tiny .008-inch (0.2-mm) mite lives in glands beneath the skin that produce an oily or waxy substance called sebum. Most people have no symptoms, but *D. brevis* can cause flare-ups of skin ailments like rosacea (which causes redness) or blepharitis (inflamed, itchy eyelids).

Follicle Mite: *Demodex folliculorum* lives in the hair follicles of your eyelashes and in pores on your nose and forehead. Its needle-sharp mouthparts pierce skin and feed on the liquid inside skin cells or on oil from sweat glands.

TERRIBLE TAPEWORM

MEET THE MONSTER

THE FLATTENED BODY OF THIS FLATWORM MAKES IT LOOK LIKE A LONG, THIN STRIP OF MASKING TAPE. But it doesn't just stick around harmlessly. It invades the intestinal tract and liver; it moves in when a person eats raw or undercooked meat containing a tapeworm egg.

ALIEN ARRIVAL

When the egg hatches, the larva burrows into the intestinal lining. The growing tapeworm absorbs digested food through its body surface. It doesn't have its own mouth or digestive system. Living in an ever-present soup of predigested food inside a host's intestines, it simply doesn't need these body parts.

Like people abducted by aliens, the victims of a tapeworm invasion often don't know that they are infected. The parasite doesn't cause serious harm, other than stealing food and sometimes causing diarrhea and nausea. People infected with a tapeworm can be treated with a worm-killing medicine.

BY THE NUMBERS

The largest human parasite, one type of tapeworm can grow up to **30 feet** (9 m) long, about twice the length of a **small car!**

CRITTER REPORT

EVOLUTION OF PARASITES

Nobody likes a mooch. Yet our bodies, homes, and the world we live in are crawling with millions of parasites—critters that mooch off other species for **their own benefit.** How did this creepy lifestyle evolve?

Scientists say that parasitism began **250 MILLION YEARS AGO,** before the Mesozoic era. You may have noticed that unlike predators, **parasites don't usually kill their hosts.** Why kill 'em when you can get your long-lasting food supply for free? In short, parasites have adapted ways to **live on or inside hosts for long periods of time,** and they move from host to host as the need to feed arises. To accomplish this, parasites tend to **"specialize,"** meaning they survive on a limited diet in a **very specific environment.** For example, head lice thrive on blood from the human scalp; a fluke lives on body tissue inside a cow's liver. The downside of specialization: If a host goes extinct, the parasite must **adapt** and find another host or **die off as well.**

DID YOU KNOW?

At least one species of tapeworm attacks the bodies of nearly every species of mammal, fish, and bird.

GROSS GUINEA WORM

MEET THE MONSTER

IN REMOTE PARTS OF AFRICA, THE GUINEA WORM (*DRACUNCULUS MEDINENSIS*, OR "LITTLE DRAGON") INVADES HUMANS WHEN THEY DRINK INFECTED POND WATER. A water flea called a Cyclops first ingests the larvae. When a person drinks the contaminated water, the Cyclops is dissolved by gastric acid in the victim's stomach. The guinea worm larvae then migrate through the intestinal wall.

ALIEN ARRIVAL

One hundred days after infestation, male and female guinea worms mate. The male dies, but the female travels into the victim's muscles. Following a year of painful infection, the female worm grows to full-adult size—two to three feet (60 to 100 cm) long and as wide as a cooked strand of spaghetti. When the worm is ready to emerge, it creates a painful blister on the human's skin. The blister causes a burning sensation so painful that the victim plunges into water to relieve it. That's when the worm emerges out of the wound. It releases a milky fluid into the water, which contains millions of larvae. And the process begins again.

There is no vaccine or drug to treat guinea worm disease. Many countries are working to wipe out the disease using insecticide in infected water and by providing clean drinking water to villages.

DID YOU KNOW?

When a guinea worm starts to exit through a wound in the feet, the rest of the worm can be pulled out a few centimeters at a time by winding it around a stick.

MANURE MONSTER

CLOSTRIDIUM DIFFICILE (C. DIFF.) ARE HARMFUL BACTERIA FOUND IN SOIL, AIR, WATER, HUMAN AND ANIMAL POOP, AND CONTAMINATED FOOD. The bacteria can cause a disease known as *Clostridium difficile* infection (CDI), which is resistant to antibiotics and causes intense pain and severe diarrhea.

ALIEN ARRIVAL

Usually the stomach has "good" bacteria that fight off *C. diff.* But when people take antibiotics for other illnesses, they kill off some of the good bacteria and allow *C. diff.* to flourish. *[Caution: Gross-out alert!]* One effective treatment is a "fecal transplant." A stool (or poop) sample from a healthy donor is collected, strained, and transplanted into the colon of an infected person. This gives healthy gut bacteria a chance to take over the bad guys.

Recently, in the United States, Dr. Ilan Youngster, a pediatric infectious disease specialist at Massachusetts General Hospital in Boston, came up with a new treatment for *C. diff.* He developed a "poop pill," a frozen capsule filled with strained human feces. For patients who can get over the "yuck factor," the pills—which are meant to be swallowed—are being studied as a safe method for restoring healthy gut bacteria.

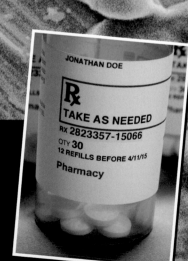

JONATHAN DOE

Rx

TAKE AS NEEDED

RX 2823357-15066
QTY 30
12 REFILLS BEFORE 4/11/15

Pharmacy

CRITTER REPORT
MICROBIOME UNDER ATTACK

Recent evidence suggests that **GUT BACTERIA** may influence the **structure of our brains** as we grow up. They may also influence our moods, behavior, and feelings as adults. Some microbes might sway our impulses to eat certain foods. **Talk about gut feelings!**

But like the biodiversity of the world, the human microbiome (the microorganisms living in our bodies) is under attack, causing possible health risks to human hosts. The **increased use of antibiotics** (which wipe out body bugs) may be causing a rise in allergies, obesity, diabetes, celiac disease, and other **health conditions.**

ATHLETE'S FOOT FUNGUS

BY THE NUMBERS

Every human being on Earth walks around with **100 trillion bacterial cells** on board—that outnumbers human cells **10 to 1!**

ALIEN ARRIVAL

Tinea pedis is a skin infection caused by a fungus (actually a mold!) that makes skin red, scaly, and itchy. Our feet pick up the fungus from damp areas like swimming pools and locker rooms. The fungus decomposes (breaks down) dead skin cells. Other symptoms that your feet are home to alien entities include stinging and burning between the toes, itchy blisters, cracked and peeling skin, and even discolored, thick, and crumbly toenails. You can drive off any uninvited fungal guests by using treatments like antifungal cream or powder, keeping feet dry, wearing big enough shoes, and changing your stinky socks daily.

ANTIFUNGAL OINTMENTS CAN HELP TREAT ITCHINESS CAUSED BY ATHLETE'S FOOT.

BUG SCIENTIST
DR. MICHELLE TRAUTWEIN

JUMPING SPIDER

DR. TRAUTWEIN IN THE AMAZON

As a kid, Michelle Trautwein wanted to be an artist, not a scientist. Then in college, as an art major, she became fascinated by the beauty of insects. She took a class on entomology (the science of bugs) and fell in love with learning about the diversity of life and evolution.

Today, Trautwein is an entomologist, or bug scientist, at the California Academy of Sciences in the United States. Recently, she made some hair-raising discoveries about bugs in our homes. "Houses on average host about 100 different arthropod species," she says. "Some of the most common [bugs] found in houses are creatures that most people have never heard of—even though we are living with them every day—like book lice and gall midges."

What inspired Trautwein to creep around on her hands and knees collecting bugs in homes? "Bugs are everywhere and people are curious about them," she says. "Our houses, like rain forests, are places that are still relatively poorly explored. There are still exciting discoveries to be made right under our noses!"

A large team of entomologists, ecologists, grad students, volunteers, and homeowners worked on the project. "Indoor expeditions are just as much work as outdoors," she says. "We wear knee pads and headlamps and spend hours searching windowsills and baseboards."

Their most important tool is a suction device called an aspirator or a pooter. It sucks up tiny insects or their body parts into a vial. Scientists then take the samples back to the lab for closer inspection under a microscope. "We mostly don't know what we've collected until we have a chance to look at things more closely," says Trautwein.

The good news: The vast majority of bugs in houses are totally harmless. "The top predators—mostly spiders—are probably helpful in keeping other populations of bugs lower," says Trautwein. She thinks of all these species as friendly roommates. "There are predators, parasites, and scavengers all living out their crazy life histories behind our walls while we sit on the couch and watch TV," she says.

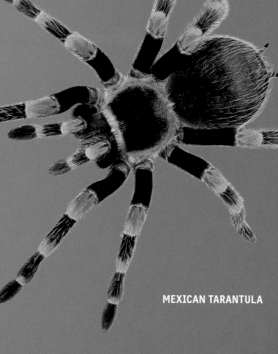

MEXICAN TARANTULA

Trautwein's favorite bug? "Right now I am loving book lice. They are close relatives of head lice, but they don't suck blood. They live in almost every house we have ever sampled—all over the world—so they are closely associated with humans. Most people have never noticed them because they are the size of a big speck of dust. They have big round noses and are absolutely adorable," she says. Spoken like a true bug lover!

At the end of the day (or night), **SPIDERS ARE HELPFUL.** They mostly eat bugs, which means **fewer pests** in our homes and gardens. Without spiders, **insect populations would explode** and our **food crops would be decimated.** Plus, spiders don't feed on humans, despite their hearty appetites.

YELLOW GARDEN SPIDER

DR. TRAUTWEIN COLLECTS SAMPLES.

UNLIKE HEAD LICE, WHICH FEAST ON BLOOD, BOOK LICE SCARF DOWN MOLD AND MILDEW ON OLD BOOKS.

BY THE NUMBERS

If you weighed **all the spiders on Earth** on a **giant scale,** they would weigh 25 million tons (22.7 million t)! By comparison, the *Titanic* weighed 52,000 tons (47,174 t). So the mass of all the spiders on Earth = 478 *Titanics*! Feeling a little sunk?

BY THE NUMBERS

The world's spiders devour between **400** and **800 million tons** (363 million and 726 million t) of prey in a year. That's **more meat than all seven billion humans** on the planet consume each year!

HOME INVADERS

MEET THE MONSTERS

OUR HOMES ARE UNDER ALIEN ATTACK! The North Carolina Museum of Natural Sciences in the United States recently completed a study of 50 homes to find out what bugs had moved in. They collected 10,000 specimens—both living and dead—and discovered as many as 100 different species of creepy critters in a single house. And not one of them paid rent.

ALIEN ARRIVAL

Bugs invade our homes to find food and shelter. They often hide out in dark basements, drainpipes, crevices behind the walls, and under the fridge! Recently, scientists discovered that some bugs are preprogrammed from birth to seek darkness. A hormone, or chemical signal, triggered by light sensors lining the bodies of insect larvae controls their preference for gloomy rooms. Darkness helps protect them from animal predators—and people with brooms.

So the next time you flip on the kitchen light and see a bug skitter behind the fridge, just remember: It was programmed for the dark side.

Stinkbugs: What's that stench? As their name suggests, stinkbugs give off a nasty odor when they get together. They produce their stench from scent glands under their abdomen.

Moth Flies: These little monsters have a thing for muck. Moth flies—aka drain flies, filter flies, or sewer flies—love to suck up the muck inside drainpipes.

Earwigs: Earwigs prefer cool, moist spaces. They sport pincers on the back of their abdomen, which they use for defense or sparring with other earwigs. They also produce a stinky liquid to scare off predators.

Dust Mites: These tiny "mite-y" vacuum cleaners suck up flakes of dead skin on our floors and in our beds. The bugs are almost invisible to the human eye, but these unseen invaders live in homes on every continent except Antarctica.

Deathwatch Beetles: To attract mates, these critters make a tapping or ticking sound that can be heard from inside the rafters of a quiet house at night. Deathwatch beetles got their ominous name from their association with all-night vigils held by the bedside of dying relatives. *Tick, tick, tick ...*

Spitting Spiders: These nocturnal arachnids spit a poisonous, gluey fluid on prey up to 0.8 inch (2 cm) away. The sticky liquid contains both spider silk and venom, which paralyzes the prey.

Silverfish: These shimmery gray insects tend to hang out in the dark, damp areas of the house, like the attic, basement, and under the bathroom and kitchen sinks. They have a bizarre diet: Dead skin, insect cadavers, hair, shampoo, glue, and leather are all on the menu.

Carpet Beetle Larvae: Like aliens traveling light-years to find food, carpet beetle larvae are miniature eating machines. Barely visible at 0.2 inch (5 mm) in length, they squirm from room to room in search of a meal, devouring dead insects, spilled pet food, fabrics, oats, flour, and even our nail clippings!

67

ATTACK OF THE ALIENS

For thousands of years, humans have looked up at the night sky and wondered: Are we alone? The first recorded sighting of a UFO—an unidentified flying object—appeared in ancient Chinese texts from the fourth century. They described a "moon boat" hovering over China every 12 years. Over the centuries, thousands of people have reported seeing eerie floating objects or unexplained lights flashing in the night sky.

Think about it: In our vast universe, our sun is one of at least 100 billion other stars. Outside our solar system, many other stars have their own planets revolving around them. Scientists have discovered more than 1,800 of these "exoplanets," and thousands more await. Could other worlds host living beings? And if they do, could the aliens be intelligent enough to reach out to us—or even attack?

Sorry, Martian lovers, but it's not likely that we'll find little green men as our neighbors.

For starters, most of those planets are gas giants, like Jupiter. They don't have solid surfaces where "monsters" can evolve, as Earth has. On the flip side, new planets are being discovered all the time, so (almost) anything's possible.

LENTICULAR CLOUDS LIKE THIS ONE MAY BE RESPONSIBLE FOR SOME "UFO" SIGHTINGS.

But what about a different kind of Martian? Those alien invaders in your body might not be so different from actual aliens after all. Scientists believe that if they do discover life on other planets, it will most likely be in the form of tiny microbes, much like those living in the extreme environments of the human gut, the deep sea, or inside Earth's crust.

One chilling example: Deep inside a South African gold mine, scientists have unearthed a mysterious treasure—microbes and worms living in water heated by the planet's interior. The dark mine, about a mile (1.6 km) deep, mimics conditions that likely exist beneath the icy surface of Mars. This discovery makes scientists hopeful that they may one day soon solve the mystery of whether extraterrestrial life exists—or ever existed—on the red planet.

BY THE NUMBERS

Between 1952 and 1969, more than **12,000 UFO sightings** were reported in the United States. Nearly all of them were identified as being **astronomical, atmospheric,** or **artificial phenomena.** About 6 percent remain "**unidentified.**"

CHAPTER 5

ANIMAL MONSTER MASH

GHOSTS, SLIME MONSTERS & MORE

Most of the time, when we face off with "monsters," they take the shape of ghouls and goblins and every other Halloween costume under the moon. We might jump in fear when we open the door to a masked trick-or-treater, but deep down we know that we are safe from harm. We might break a sweat or feel our heart pounding, but we know that monsters aren't real.

Humans have been drawn to monsters throughout time— from ancient Greek tales of the snake-headed Medusa to today's sparkly teenage vampires. Some psychologists say that thrill-seeking humans are attracted to monsters because the confrontation allows us to show how brave our minds can be over our body's instinct to run away. Sometimes our thrills over- come the chills and our human curiosity takes over our fears.

This chapter explores a "monster mash" of some of nature's most fantastic beasts. And guess what? They are all REAL! Can you handle it?

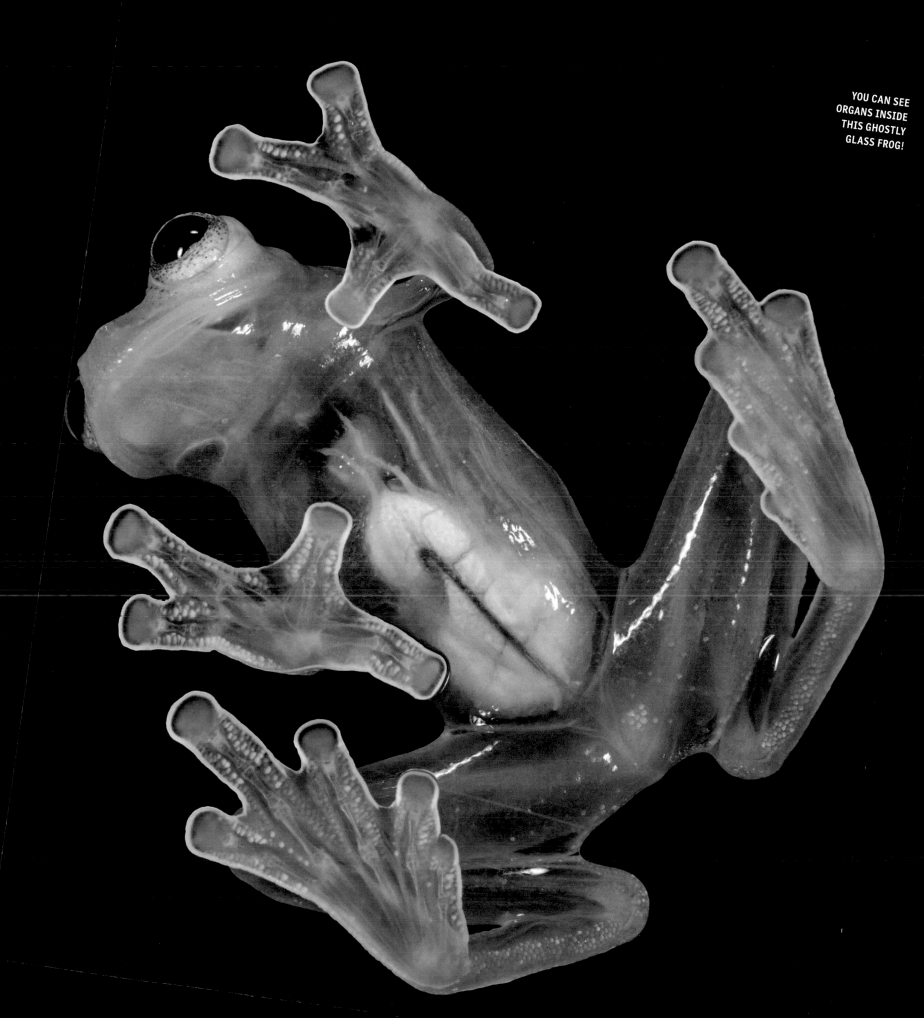

YOU CAN SEE
ORGANS INSIDE
THIS GHOSTLY
GLASS FROG!

Scientists think that glass frogs are a **HELPFUL BIO-INDICATOR,** a species that provides clues about the **health of its environment.** As global **climate changes,** some rain forests where the frogs live are **becoming dry.** Scientists keep an eye on the frogs, which need moisture to thrive, to see how **global warming** may be impacting their habitat.

GLASSY GHOST FROG

MEET THE MONSTER

GLASS FROGS, LIME GREEN, QUARTER-SIZE AMPHIBIANS, HAVE TRANSLUCENT (SEMI SEE-THROUGH) BELLIES. When they leap, you can see some of their internal organs, like their intestines and liver! You can even watch their heart beating inside! *Ba-dump ba-dump ba-dump!* **Some species have green-colored bones, which you can see inside their arms and legs. These eerie frogs, which come out at night, live in the rain forests of Central and South America.**

FREAKY FACTS

The froggy "ghosts" don't float. But during breeding season, the frogs hop down from the treetops of the rain forest canopy to live near rivers and streams. Females lay a clutch of eggs on the underside of a leaf. They stick them in place with a gooey, jellylike substance. Male glass frogs often sleep by day next to the eggs to protect them. They squeak and wrestle to keep predators away. They may even kick away wasps that get too close.

No one is sure why these frogs, scientific name Centrolenidae, are see-through. It might be for camouflage, helping them blend in with their surroundings like a ghost. What's more, the spotted green dots on the male's back may resemble eggs and help confuse predators, keeping them away from the real loot. Spooooky!

DID YOU KNOW?

The newly discovered ghost octopus could already be in danger! The females lay their eggs on sponges, which anchor themselves to rocks containing precious metals. To retrieve the metals, some mining companies are planning to turn huge patches of the seafloor into underwater mines. Removing the rocks could threaten the sponges, which means no landing site for ghost octopus eggs. That may put future ghost generations at risk.

MEET THE MONSTER

THIS SPOOKY SPECIES, CALLED THE GHOST OCTOPUS, WAS DISCOVERED IN THE DEEP SEA OFF THE COAST OF HAWAII, U.S.A. Found by a submarine robot named *Deep Discoverer* at 13,123 feet (4,000 m) below the surface, it is the deepest-dwelling finless octopus the world has ever seen.

FREAKY FACTS

The ghost octopus has several adaptations for living in the deep. For starters, it is a gelatinous blob with very few muscles—building muscles requires food for energy, and food is scarce in the deep. The octopus also has tiny eyes, which may be able to spot bioluminescent prey.

Scientists have also learned that the female ghost octopus has an unusual parenting strategy. (Get out the tissues, folks. This is sad.) She attaches her clutch of quarter-size eggs to the stalk of a dead sponge and then wraps her body around the eggs to protect them. Then she waits for them to hatch. And waits. And waits. Without food. FOR YEARS. Once the eggs hatch, the ghostly mom withers away and dies. The mama ghost sacrifices herself to save her babies. Not just *boo*, but *boo-hoo!* (Sorry, peeps, we warned you!)

BY THE NUMBERS

A female ghost octopus lays 30 eggs at a time.

TASTY TOAD

MEET THE MONSTER

THESE WARTY CANE TOADS, WHICH CAN BE FOUND FROM THE SOUTHWESTERN UNITED STATES DOWN TO SOUTH AMERICA, GIVE OFF A POISON THAT CAN KILL ANIMALS TRYING TO EAT THEM. Some of their natural predators, including caimans, snakes, eels, and fish, have either developed immunity to their venom or have learned to avoid the parts of the toad that give off poison.

FREAKY FACTS

Not long ago, researchers noticed that the eggs of the cane toad, *Rhinella marina,* were disappearing. At first they thought that freshwater crocodiles must be feasting on the toad eggs. Then they made a startling discovery: The toads were slurping down their own kind! Tadpoles of these poisonous toads chow down fresh batches of eggs of their own species! Even midsize toads wriggle their toes to lure smaller toads and then—*gulp!*— swallow them whole.

Scientists cite three motivations for this cannibalistic behavior: First, it speeds up development of the tadpoles into toads. With more energy from food, they grow and turn into toads faster. Second, it eliminates future rivals. The female lays thousands of eggs at a time. If they all hatch, the toad population would be vast, and there would be less food to go around. Third, because the toads are toxic to other species (but not their own), eating their own kind opens up an untouched food source. It's a toad-eat-toad world!

HORROR OR HELPER?

Not all toads are **CANNIBALISTIC KILLERS.** But they all play an important role in the **food chain.** They eat insects and other invertebrates, and they are prey for fish, birds, reptiles, mammals, and other amphibians. Many toad and frog populations have declined since the 1970s due to **habitat destruction, pesticide use, pollution, disease,** and **overcollection** for food and pets. We need to help preserve our hoppy friends.

CANNIBAL CRICKETS

MEET THE MONSTER

IMAGINE STEPPING OUT OF LINE ON YOUR WAY TO LUNCH. Suddenly the kid behind you takes a bite out of your leg. Horror movie? No, just life in the lunch line of Mormon crickets.

BY THE NUMBERS
A **swarm** of Mormon crickets can stretch **half a mile** (0.8 km) long!

FREAKY FACTS

Mormon crickets, *Anabrus simplex,* which live in the western United States, march in a single line toward new food sources. They can't fly, but they can hop and crawl as far as a mile (1.6 km) in a day. But if one Mormon cricket steps out of line, the other bugs in the swarm will eat it.

Here's why: Hungry crickets need protein and salt. Their typical diet of 400 plant species lacks those nutrients. But other crickets—those that don't stay in line or that tend to be slowpokes—make a tasty and salty protein snack. Another theory is that the nips and bites from crickets behind them keep the swarm moving forward quickly. *"Ouch! Stop! I'm marching! I'm marching!"* If that's not enough, some hungry Mormon crickets will even eat their own exoskeletons, which fall off when they molt.

ONE MORMON CRICKET FEASTS ON ANOTHER.

HORROR OR HELPER?

MALE MORMON CRICKETS are surprisingly helpful to their mates, a unique trait for insects. The male gives the female a **big blob of food** to eat as part of the mating process. The generous blob is **27 percent of the male's body weight,** the same as a 150-pound (68-kg) man giving his female partner a **40-pound (18.1-kg) chunk of flesh** as a gift.

BEASTLY BLOB

MEET THE MONSTER

THIS GOOPY CREATURE IS A SINGLE-CELLED ORGANISM THAT SOMETIMES GATHERS WITH OTHER SLIME MOLDS INTO A BIG OOZING BLOB. Also known as the many-headed slime mold, its other nicknames include wolf's milk, bubblegum, and pretzel. Some people have mistaken the pulsating jellylike mass for dog vomit!

DID YOU KNOW?

Slime molds have many alien features. They look like a blobby, foamy mess. But if you try to chop them up, they will pull themselves back together! Even without a brain, slime molds can navigate and avoid obstacles.

FREAKY FACTS

Slime molds feed on bacteria and other microorganisms found in dead plant matter. They lack the green pigment chlorophyll, so they come in many colors—except snot green, contrary to what you might expect from slime!

When life is good (that is, when they have enough food and light), they live as independent amoeba-like cells, engulfing bacteria and fungi for meals. But when conditions get rough, they send out chemical signals to other slime mold cells to join forces. It's like an alien sending out signals to gather the troops. Together, a micro-army of hundreds of thousands of cells mobilizes to form a newly united slimy structure known as a slug. (It's different from the brown slugs, which are gastropod mollusks, that creep along your sidewalk leaving a sticky trail.) The slime-mold slug oozes like a single organism, moving toward food or light like an unstoppable blob of horror.

SLIME MOLDS COME IN MANY COLORS (EXCEPT GREEN).

BY THE NUMBERS

Slime molds can **move** at a rate of a quarter inch (6 mm) an hour.

MUCUS MONSTER

•••••○ HORROR OR HELPER? ○•••••

Hagfish **SLIME** is very strong. It's made of tens of thousands of **very thin protein threads,** 100 times thinner than human hair. Scientists think hagfish slime could be used to **weave super-strong fabric** to make **bulletproof vests** or even **tissues!** Imagine wiping your slimy snot with a sheet of hagfish mucus! *Gross!*

MEET THE MONSTER

LET'S SAY YOU'RE A SLIPPERY, BONELESS, AND JAWLESS FISH THAT LOOKS LIKE AN EEL. You're swimming around looking for a meal in the deep sea around 5,600 feet (1,707 m) beneath the ocean's surface. Predators, including hungry sharks, are lurking in the dark. How do you protect yourself? With slime!

FREAKY FACTS

Hagfish secrete globs of sticky mucus from glands that run along their body. The gross goop makes attackers gag and may also clog their gills.

To clean the slime off its own body, the hagfish ties itself in a knot and then scrapes off the gooey stuff as it unties itself. To clear the slime from its single nostril, it sneezes into the sea. *Gesundheit!*

To hide from predators, hagfish, scientific name Myxinidae, nose-dive into the muddy seafloor. How do these monsters breathe under cover? A network of tiny blood vessels might allow them to breathe through their skin while they're buried in mud.

Hagfish are also a kind of creepy cleanup crew. They mostly feed on dead or dying creatures on the seafloor. When hagfish find a meal, they burrow deep into its flesh, face first, and devour the carcass from the inside out. These dudes have been trolling for dead critters in the ocean's graveyard for 330 million years.

MOUTH-WATERING MOM

BY THE NUMBERS

About 120 species of caecilians live on four continents. The smaller species are about three inches (7.6 cm) long, while the largest species, *Caecilia thompsoni*, from Colombia, stretches five feet (1.5 m) long!

MEET THE MONSTER

SOME MOMS WILL DO *ANYTHING* FOR THEIR BABIES. A mother caecilian, a wormlike amphibian that lives underground, engages in matriphagy, feeding her own body to her offspring. In some caecilian species, the offspring are born live; in others, they hatch from eggs. After a few months, the mother lies still as her little ones line up by her side. No, it's not story time. It's lunchtime—and the mom is lunch!

FREAKY FACTS

When juvenile caecilians are mature enough, their mom's outer layer of skin swells with fat. With rows of tiny specialized teeth—some blunt for scraping and others hooked for grabbing—the young caecilians peel their mom like a carrot from head to tail!

Within 10 minutes, they have skinned their mom alive and eaten her! *"Mmmm, such a yummy mommy!"* She sacrificed her own life so the next generation could live. It might seem like a gut-turning way of investing in her offspring's future, but it gives them the nutrition they need to develop and grow in their muddy underworld where food can be hard to find. Maybe mama caecilians should win the "Monster Mom of the Year Award"!

DID YOU KNOW?

Some caecilians are blind, while others have tiny eyes under their skin.

HEADS OR TAILS? HARD TO TELL WITH THESE LIMBLESS AMPHIBIANS.

SPEWING SPIDER

MEET THE MONSTER

THE FEMALE VELVET SPIDER, *STEGODYPHUS LINEATUS*, **LIVES IN DRY MEDITERRANEAN HABITATS AND GIVES IT ALL UP FOR HER KIDS. The** mother spins a silk disk containing 70 to 80 eggs. Meanwhile, her intestines begin to dissolve. Once the eggs hatch, the mother punctures the disk, letting the baby spiders emerge. To feed them, the mother starts to—literally—puke her guts out.

FREAKY FACTS

Young velvet spiders feast on their mother's liquefied insides! In several hours, they devour 96 percent of their mother's mass. All that remains is her heart and a hollow exoskeleton.

Can this get any creepier? Why, of course it can! In a related species called *Stegodyphus dumicola,* other female spiders arrive to help feed the young. These selfless helpers throw up more food for the babies. Their previously chewed food supply increases the chances that the spiderlings will survive. But the helpers are doomed! The ungrateful young spiders kill and eat these female helpers, too. After feeding, the babies swell like tiny balloons. They grow and molt (shed their exoskeletons) and skitter away.

HORROR OR HELPER?

PARASITIC WASPS and **ANTS** sometimes **feed on the spiders' eggs.** If this happens before the female begins to **digest her intestines,** she may lay another clutch of eggs.

79

QUIVERING QUILLS

MEET THE MONSTER

WELCOME TO FRIGHT NIGHT! The crested porcupine, *Hystrix cristada,* has a hair-raising habit when it goes out after dark. It hunts for skeletons and digs up their bones! Then it hauls them back to its underground den. What does this prickly critter do with piles of bones? It gnaws on them to file down its long, sharp teeth that keep on growing throughout the rodent's life.

CRESTED PORCUPINES HUNT FOR BONES AT NIGHT.

PORCUPINE QUILLS SNAG SKIN LIKE FISHHOOKS!

FREAKY FACTS

A porcupine probably isn't the creature you think of when you picture a deep, dark night, but trust us—you don't want to get close. When a predator comes too near, the porcupine may stomp its feet, raise its quills, and charge the intruder rear end first, where its short quills are sharpest. It's been known to skewer attackers, including lions, hyenas, leopards, and even humans! The porcupine's tail also has hollow quills that rattle when they vibrate, producing a hissing sound. Not something you want to hear in the dark woods!

WAILING WOLVES

MEET THE MONSTER

FORGET WEREWOLVES—REAL WOLVES IN THE WILD ARE CHILLING ENOUGH. A hair-raising howl sends shivers down your spine. From the pitch-black, two glowing eyes emerge, and an enormous animal comes into view.

LIKE A FINGERPRINT, A WOLF'S HOWL IS UNIQUE, ALLOWING OTHER MEMBERS OF THE PACK (AND SCIENTISTS) TO TELL THEM APART.

BY THE NUMBERS

Most wolf packs have about **10 wolves**, but some can have as many as **30**.

FREAKY FACTS

Humans have long feared wolves for their incredible strength and ferocious fangs. A wolf can take down a large elk or moose and scarf 20 pounds (9 kg) of meat in a single meal. That's like chowing down 80 large burgers at once! These incredible predators have even inspired stories about werewolves and villainous fairy-tale monsters. But unlike werewolves, real wolves aren't monsters; they are complex creatures with close family groups.

Although werewolves tend to be loners, real wolves hunt and travel in packs at night. The leader of the pack is the alpha male, who fiercely protects his family. Each pack guards its territory against intruders and will even kill another wolf that threatens the pack.

Wolves also have a surprising social system that they act out with body language. For example, when one wolf submits to a stronger wolf, it will crouch, whimper, tuck in its tail, roll over, or lick the other wolf's mouth. To show dominance, a wolf will growl or draw its ears back on its head. Wolves also dance and bow for play.

And although a werewolf's howl might frighten the locals, real wolves' howls scare away invaders and help wolves track other pack members when they're apart.

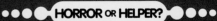

HORROR or HELPER?

In the 19th and 20th centuries, **HUNTERS KILLED WOLVES** by the thousands because the predators were misunderstood as **cattle-killing pests.** Today they are **protected and are making a comeback.** Wolves play an important role in **maintaining the balance in the food web.**

WOLF MAN
DR. L. DAVID MECH

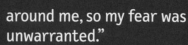

Since the story of Little Red Riding Hood, which first appeared in writing in 1697, people have expressed fear of the "Big Bad Wolf." Today wolf attacks on humans are extremely rare. Because of hunting and habitat destruction, wolves virtually disappeared from the lower 48 U.S. states in the 20th century, with the exception of northern Minnesota. However, due to conservation and efforts to reintroduce wolves into the wild, about 60,000 wolves now live in North America.

Dr. L. David Mech (pronounced "Meech") has been studying wolves and their prey for about six decades. As a child, he loved the great outdoors. "When I was a teenager I observed animals like muskrats, mink, and foxes and developed an interest in how animals live," he says.

Today Mech studies wolves in national parks like Yellowstone by trapping them and attaching radio collars. Then he follows them and observes them from a small airplane. He also tracks wolves on his computer.

"Most wolves are very afraid of humans," says Mech. "The only place in the world where they are not is in Ellesmere Island." Wolves in that remote region of northern Canada have had almost no contact with humans. Mech spent his summers there between 1986 and 2010 (except 1999), camping out on the tundra and closely observing a pack of arctic wolves with a photographer.

The duo observed that the wolves would howl in the morning just before a hunt. The parents also howled to rein in their pups. Because they travel long distances, wolves howl to communicate with each other and to warn off competitors. "To wolves, howling is the glue that holds the family together," Mech says. He even got so comfortable with the pack that he joined the howling!

An adult wolf once snuck up on Mech. "He was a few feet behind me but I didn't see him," he recalls. "For about half a minute I was concerned that he might try to explore me by nipping me. Then if I were to jump up, I thought I might trigger his attack instinct. But he merely walked around me, so my fear was unwarranted."

Mech and the photographer once stayed up for 24 hours to observe the pack. They observed many previously unseen behaviors, like the mom regurgitating (vomiting) her meal to feed her pups and the pups competing for food.

The researcher's patience also paid off toward the end of summer. Mech had front-row seats to watch the pack hunting a herd of furry muskoxen and snagging a calf. Although the attack was brutal and bloody, Mech was mesmerized by the rare spectacle. Describing his summers with wolves, Mech says, "It was a dream come true."

SCIENTISTS FITTED THIS WOLF IN YELLOWSTONE WITH A RADIO COLLAR FOR TRACKING.

DR. DAVID MECH (LEFT)
AND A GRAD STUDENT
USE A RADIO ANTENNA
TO TRACK A WOLF PACK.

A SCALY ESCAPE

MEET THE MONSTER

THE GRAYISH FISH-SCALE GECKO IS A MASTER OF ILLUSION. Normally, it blends in nicely with rocks and bark, avoiding all notice. But on rare occasions when its disguise fails, this Houdini-like creature has a shocking way of escaping. When attacked, the lizard literally jumps out of its outer layer of skin, sheds it scales, and slips away naked! You can even see its spine and its blood vessels throbbing inside its pink-flesh body. One scientist compares the bare gecko to a raw chicken breast. *Ewww!*

FREAKY FACTS

This gory getaway may seem grotesque but it apparently doesn't harm the lizard. The scales regenerate in a few weeks. Scientists discovered the species, *Geckolepis megalepis*, in Madagascar. They observed that if a predator tries to bite the lizard, the attacker ends up with a mouthful of scales as the gecko runs away. The scales aren't used as armor but rather as a decoy or distraction. *"Bleh, scales! Hey, where'd he go?"*

The reason that the geckos are able to undress so quickly: Each scale is attached to the gecko's skin along predefined "tear zones," much like the perforations that allow you to pull apart postage stamps in a sheet. Amazingly, this "ripped" critter can put itself back together again.

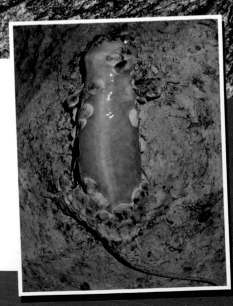

WITHOUT SCALES, THE GECKO LOOKS LIKE RAW CHICKEN.

HIDDEN HORROR

MEET THE MONSTER

HEY, IS THAT TREE WATCHING ME? Welcome to the haunted forest of the tawny frogmouth. This bird blends in so well with its bark backdrop that you may almost miss it. A native of Australia, the tawny frogmouth is nocturnal. To protect itself by day, it sits completely still, closes its large yellow eyes, stretches its neck, and tamps down its feathers so it looks like a dead tree branch. *"Nobody here but us branches. Move along!"*

FREAKY FACTS

But look out little rodents, lizards, and insects! As the sun goes down, tawny frogmouths spring to life. They pounce from their perch, snatching unwary prey in their sharp beaks. They may also catch moths in mid-flight.

As if being a terror in disguise weren't enough, this bird, *Podargus strigoides,* has a few other creepy tricks under its wing. In cold winter months, the forest food supply shrinks. The tawny frogmouth can live only a short time on stored fat. So it spends part of its winter days in a deadened state called torpor. The bird's heart rate and metabolism slow down. That conserves energy and lowers the bird's body temperature. (Torpor is different from hibernation in that torpor lasts only a few hours at a time, while hibernation lasts several months.) After a few hours, the "dead" bird comes back to life, ready to catch unsuspecting victims!

A TAWNY FROGMOUTH STAYS HIDDEN BY MIMICKING A BRANCH.

BY THE NUMBERS

During **nighttime torpor** (a low-energy state), the tawny frogmouth's body temperature drops as much as 50°F (a change of 28°C).

HEADLESS HORRORS

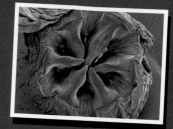

COCKROACH GUT

MEET THE MONSTER

FLICK ON THE KITCHEN LIGHT AT NIGHT AND WATCH THEM SCURRY—FEW BUGS CAUSE AS MANY SHRIEKS AS COCKROACHES. About 4,000 species of cockroaches live around the world, with 70 species in the United States alone. They have been around for more than 350 million years, and many people say roaches will outlive us all.

FREAKY FACTS

Cockroaches can be hard to kill. They live on few necessities and can survive almost a month without food or two weeks without water. A roach could survive 45 minutes without air. And get this: Its respiratory system doesn't require a head. Nerve clusters throughout their body act like a brain. (That's why roaches continue to squirm even if their head is chopped off.)

But there's another reason they can get crushed and keep going. Their exoskeletons are made up of overlapping plates connected by an elastic membrane. The plates are strong but flexible, so when a roach is squashed or escapes through a crack in the wall, its body is flattened while the energy shifts to its legs. Spines on its feet help the squashed little monster stick to surfaces while it skitters away. *"Missed again!"*

HORROR OR HELPER?

Some scientists think we should all drink **COCKROACH MILK** as the **new superfood!** Not technically "milk," the protein crystals found in the guts of cockroaches pack **four times the nutrients** of cow's milk. And because roaches are oh so plentiful, scientists think they may hold the key to feeding the world's **growing population** in the future. Of course, milking **millions of cockroaches** doesn't seem practical (don't try this at home!). So scientists are trying to copy the **GENES** responsible for making the protein crystals and reproduce them in a lab.

DID YOU KNOW?

Roaches can sustain 15 times the radiation that would kill a human because their cells divide more slowly.

CONSTANT CRITTER

MEET THE MONSTER

THIS MICROSCOPIC CREATURE WITH EIGHT LIMBS LOOKS LIKE IT BELONGS IN A SCI-FI THRILLER. One of the world's smallest animals, tardigrades (also called water bears) live across seven continents in every environment. They average about .02 inch (0.5 mm) in length, about the size of a grain of sand. Virtually indestructible, tardigrades have been found at the ocean's depths, inside hot springs, and even on the frozen top of Mount Everest, the world's highest peak.

FREAKY FACTS

To test the little monsters' might, scientists sent some tardigrades into space on a rocket for 10 days. When the critters returned to Earth, most were still alive! How did they survive a journey into outer space exposed to extreme cold and lack of air—an environment that would kill a human in seconds? Like yeast or brine shrimp (also known as "sea monkeys"), tardigrades can survive extreme drying. When their environment dries up, so do they. They can lose nearly all of their water and remain in suspended animation until they are rehydrated days or months later.

Recently, scientists discovered that when tardigrades, scientific name Tardigrada, dry out, they produce a protein that protects molecules in their cells as if they were sealed in a glass coating. The molecules remain in a suspended state until the tardigrades are rehydrated. Water melts the glasslike proteins and the molecules begin to function again. The tardigrades flex their legs and spring back to life like wet sponges with limbs. Like monsters from a horror movie, these are creatures that keep coming back.

NIGHT OF THE WEREWOLF

Which night creature in mythological folklore gives you the creeps? With their tendency to shape-shift from human to wolflike beast, the bloodthirsty werewolf has sent shivers up the spines of those who fear the night for over two thousand years. Here's how werewolves came to "life"!

The term "werewolf" comes from Old English, meaning "man-wolf." Like real wolves, mythical werewolves had incredible strength, super speed, powerful senses, clawlike fingernails, and a vicious bite. The belief in lycanthropy, the mythological folklore of werewolves, dates back to the first century B.C. In ancient Greek culture, a king named Lycaon was a human who was transformed into a wolf by the god Zeus as a punishment for a crime.

In the Middle Ages, stories of werewolves spread through villages like wildfire. In these folktales, men would turn into werewolves by wearing wolf skin, drinking rainwater from the footprint of a wolf, or by slurping water from an enchanted stream. In Germany and France, stories spread that a person could turn into a werewolf by sleeping outdoors on a certain night in summer under a full moon. These wolf-men would turn other people into hairy wolves by biting them. In some cultures, women also became werewolves.

In the 1300s to 1600s, werewolves were thought to be linked to witches. Like suspected witches, tens of thousands of accused werewolves were put on trial and killed in "witch hunts." One theory as to why people believed in werewolves: a fear of the unknown. An infection from rabies, caused by a bite from a rabid animal, may have sickened people and caused them to behave like wild animals. (Today, rabies infection can be cured with a vaccine.) People likely connected this misunderstood phenomenon with their natural fear of the dark, where real wolves prowled.

Many accused werewolves sought cures for their "ailment," which often included useless and painful surgeries or harmful herbs or medicines. Because werewolves were thought to dislike metal (which is associated with the moon), a silver bullet was thought to be the only surefire way to stop a werewolf. Over time, these tales have inspired dozens of hair-raising books, movies, and pop songs about werewolves. Where will they invade next?

CRITTER REPORT

NIGHT VISION

How do creatures of the night **SEE IN THE DARK?** For starters, nocturnal animals tend to have huge eyes for their body size. Owl eyes are similar in volume to human eyes, but an owl's eyes cover half the space of its skull! To be comparable, a person's eyes would have to be the size of a six-inch (15.2-cm) saucer and weigh two pounds (0.9 kg) each. *"What big eyes you have!"*

Night creatures also have pupils that expand to cover most of the front of their eye to let in maximum light. (The pupil is the dark center that opens or closes like a camera shutter to control the amount of light that enters the eye.) Bigger pupils allow animals to spot prey far away—even when the sun goes down.

Finally, many nocturnal animals have a mirrorlike layer of tissue behind the retina that reflects light back to the retina. This gives the night critter's eyes a second chance to see a little rodent or other prey running by. It also makes their eyes glow when you shine a flashlight! Yikes!

NOCTURNAL TARSIERS HAVE ENORMOUS EYES.

IN THIS ILLUSTRATION, WEREWOLVES HOWL AT THE MOON LIKE REAL WOLVES.

TALES OF HUMANLIKE WOLVES (SEEN HERE IN AN ILLUSTRATION OF LITTLE RED RIDING HOOD) HAVE EXISTED FOR CENTURIES.

YOU SURVIVED!

You've made it! You **FACED YOUR FEARS** and **SURVIVED** the world's creepiest zombifying, blood-slurping, gut-loving, poison-packing, mucus-spewing, and **DEATH-DEFYING MONSTERS.** Are you brave enough to **EXPLORE ON YOUR OWN?** Remember, the best way to investigate fiends in the field is with a friend. Make sure you **SHARE** your favorite **"YIKES"** and **"LIKES."** And tread lightly out there! You never know who— or what—you may disturb!

CONCLUSION

THE LARVAE OF *COTESIA CONGREGATA*, A PARASITIC WASP, EMERGE FROM AN INFECTED CATERPILLAR.

GLOSSARY

FIRE SALAMANDER

adaptation The process by which an organism changes over time to become better fit to survive in its environment

amoeba A freshwater or marine parasitic single-celled organism

amphibian A cold-blooded vertebrate with no scales that lives on land and water

anesthetic A substance that stops pain

annelid A segmented worm

antibiotic A medicine that stops the growth of or destroys microorganisms

arachnid A wingless, carnivorous arthropod with eight legs and no antennae

arthropod An animal with no spine, six or more jointed legs, and often a tough outer shell

bacterium (pl. bacteria) A microscopic single-celled living organism

barbel A sensory tentacle

bioluminescence The creation of light by a living organism

carnivore An organism that mainly or exclusively eats meat

REEF OCTOPUS

cephalopod A mollusk whose legs are attached to its head

crustacean An aquatic arthropod with a body covered by a hard shell or crust

cyst A closed sac with a protective wall of tissue containing fluid

decompose To break down into parts or elements

echolocation A sonar-like system that bats and other animals use to detect and locate objects by sending out high-pitched sounds that reflect off the objects and return to the animals' ears or other sensory receptors

entomologist A scientist who studies entomology

entomology The branch of science dealing with insects

enzyme A protein in living cells

exoskeleton An external skeleton that protects the bodies of certain animals

fungus (pl. fungi) An organism that lives by decomposing and absorbing the organic material in which it grows

gene A segment of DNA that provides the instructions for hereditary characteristics

hemolymph A fluid in the body of invertebrates that functions as blood

LEOPARD

KITE BUTTERFLY

hydrothermal vent An opening in Earth's crust under the sea through which ocean water is heated by magma

larva The immature, wingless feeding stage of an insect that undergoes metamorphosis

lycanthropy Mythological folklore of werewolves

magma Molten rock within or beneath Earth's crust

mammal A vertebrate that has hair, nourishes its young with milk, and gives birth to live young

matriphagy The process in which organisms feed on their own mother

metamorphosis The change in an organism's form from one stage to the next

microbiome The totality of microorganisms living on or in the human body or in another environment

molt To cast off or shed feathers, skin, or exoskeleton in the process of renewal

nematocyst A specialized venom-packed cell that can sting and paralyze prey

nocturnal Active at night

paleontologist A scientist who studies fossils

parasite An organism that lives on or in another organism, known as a host

parasitologist A scientist who studies parasites

proboscis A long flexible snout

pupa An insect in the immobile, nonfeeding, transforming stage of metamorphosis

radula tooth A harpoon-like structure in the mouth of some mollusks

regenerate To renew or restore

regurgitate To vomit

siphonophore A colony of marine organisms working together

sporocyst A stage in the development of trematodes

stool Fecal matter

translucent Permitting light to pass through

vertebrate Having a backbone or spinal column

FIND OUT MORE

Books

Carson, Mary Kay. *The Bat Scientists.* Houghton Mifflin Books for Children, 2010.

Jenkins, Martin. *Informania: Vampires.* Candlewick Press, 1998.

Johnson, Rebecca L. *Zombie Makers: True Stories of Nature's Undead.* Millbrook Press, 2012.

Marrin, Albert. *Little Monsters: The Creatures That Live on Us and in Us.* Dutton Children's Books, 2011.

Swanson, Jennifer. *Body Bugs: Invisible Creatures Lurking Inside You.* Capstone Press, 2012.

Traer, Scott. *Nocturne: Creatures of the Night.* Princeton Architectural Press, 2014.

Web

Interview with Anand Varma, nature photographer. proof.nationalgeographic.com/2014/10/31/catching-zombies-in-the-act-how-to-picture-parasites

"Mindsuckers," by Carl Zimmer, photographs by Anand Varma, National Geographic, November 2014. ngm.nationalgeographic.com/2014/11/mindsuckers/zimmer-text

CREDITS

GI: Getty Images; MP: Minden Pictures; NGC: National Geographic Creative; SS: Shutterstock

Cover: (CTR), Anand Varma/NGC; (UP RT), Helmut Corneli/Alamy; (LO LE), Alexander Semenov/GI; (LO RT), Anand Varma/NGC; **Back cover:** (CTR LE), Anand Varma/NGC; (UP LE), VitalisG/GI; (LO), Kelvin Aitken/VWPics via AP Images; (CTR RT), Photo Researchers/GI; (UP CTR), Gerry Ellis/Digital Vision; **Spine:** Oksanabratanova/Dreamstime; **Front matter:** 1, David Doubilet/NGC; 2-3, Anand Varma/NGC; 4 (LO RT), scooperdigital/GI; 4 (LO LE), Anand Varma/NGC; 5, Anand Varma/NGC; **Chapter 1:** 6-7, Anand Varma/NGC; 8, Maekawa Takayuki/Nature Production/MindenPictures; 8 (CTR LE), BlackCatPhotos/GI; 8 (LO), Jan van Duinen/MiS/MP; 9, Anand Varma/NGC; 11, Anand Varma/NGC; 10 (UP), Anand Varma/NGC; 10-11 (CTR), Anand Varma/GI; 11 (UP), Rod Williams/NPL/Minden Images; 12 (UP RT), Anand Varma/NGC; 12 (CTR), Anand Varma/NGC; 13, Anand Varma/NGC; 13 (LO LE), Anand Varma/NGC; 13 (LO RT), Anand Varma/NGC; 14, Anand Varma/NGC; 15, Slobodan Kunevski/SS; 15 (LO), D. Kucharski K. Kucharska/SS; 15 (LE), Anest/GI; 16-17, zsv3207/GI; 17 (UP), Dr_Microbe/GI; 18, Anand Varma/NGC; 19, Frank Hecker/Alamy; 20-21, Hector Hyppolite/Photo © Gerald Bloncourt/Bridgeman Images; 21 (UP), leolintang/GI; 21 (Water), fotomak/SS; 21 (Can), Hekla/SS; 21 (Flashlight and radio), Guy J. Sagi/SS; 21 (Duct tape), Feng Yu/Dreamstime; 21 (Passport), photodisc; 21 (First aid kit), Mega Pixel/SS; **Chapter 2:** 22-23, Matthew Cicanese; 24 (LE), dimid_86/SS; 24-25, Dieter Hawlan/SS; 24 (LO), Dr. Fiona Cross; 25 (UP), Janos Csongor Kerekes/GI; 25 (LO), Andrew Mayovskyy/SS; 26-27, Barry Mansell/NPL/MP; 26 (LO), Joel Sartore, National Geographic Photo Ark/NGC; 28 (LO), Michael and Patricia Fogden/MP; 28 (UP), Barcroft Media/Contributor/GI; 29 (LE), John B. Carnett/Bonnier Corporation via GI; 29 (Helmet) Love Silhouette/SS; 29 (Boots), Nicole Gordine/SS; 29 (Gloves), photodisc; 29 (Flashlight), photodisc; 29 (Camera), Maxxyustas/Dreamstime.com; 29 (Respirator), Coprid/SS; 30 (UP), Jelger Herder/Buiten-beeld/MP; 30 (CTR), James L. Amos/NGC; 30 (LO), James L. Amos/NGC; 31, szefei/GI; 31 (RT), VitalisG/GI; 32 (CTR), Marcel Langelaan/Buiten-beeld/MP; 32, Santiago Urquijo/GI; 32 (LO LE), ArtBoyMB/GI; 32 (LO), BSIP/UIG/GI; 33, Dzmitry Kliapitski/Alamy; 33 (LE), Hulton Archive/GI; 33 (LO), Stephen Dalton/Science Source; 34 (UP), Elena Gladkaya/Alamy Stock Photo; 34 (LO), Leemage/GI; 35, Granamour Weems Collection/Alamy; **Chapter 3:** 36-37, Georgette Douwma/NPL/MP; 38, Wolfgang Poelzer/GI; 39, Muriel Duhau/Biosphoto/MP; 39 (LO), Norbert Wu/MP; 40-41, Kelvin Aitken/VWPics via AP Images; 40, Awashima Marine Park/GI; 41, Kelvin Aitken/VWPics via AP Images; 42 (UP), Randall Scott/NGC; 42 (LO), by wildestanimal/GI; 43 (LO), Manu San Felix/NGC; 43 (UP), Manu San Felix/NGC; 44, Jurgen Freund/Nature Picture Library/Alamy; 45 (LO), Sean Chinn @greatwhitesean/Alamy; 45, imageBROKER/Alamy; 46 (UP), Alexander Semenov/GI; 46 (LO), Brian J. Skerry/NGC; 46-47, Alexander Semenov/GI; 48 (UP), Paulo de Oliveira/NHPA/Photoshot/Newscom; 48 (LE), Reinhard Dirscherl/GI; 48 (RT), AP Photo/Tsunemi Kubodera of the National Science Museum of Japan, HO; 49, David Shale/NPL/MP; 49, Dr. Ken MacDonald/Science Source; 50, Steve Downer/Science Source; 50 (RT), Steve Downer/Science Source; 51 (LO), Kelvin Aitken/VWPics/Alamy; 51 (UP), Paulo de Oliveira/NHPA/Photoshot/Newscom; 52-53, GI INC/NGC; 54 (UP), Sarin Images/Granger - All rights reserved; 54 (LO), North Wind Picture Archives/Alamy; 55, Stocktrek Images, Inc./Alamy; **Chapter 4:** 56-57, Matt Cicanese; 58, Science Picture Co/GI; 58-59, Blue_Cutler/GI3d Render of Dust Mite. Allergy House Hygiene Bed; 59 (UP LE), Steve Gschmeissner/Science Photo Library; 59 (UP RT), Sciepro/GI; 60, Sciepro/GI; 61, Karen Kasmauski//GI; 62, Photo Researchers/GI; 63, PhotoAlto/Odilon Dimier/GI; 62 (LO), Burlingham/SS; 64 (UP CTR), Tomatito/SS; 64 (UP RT), Rob Nelson @UntamedScience; 64 (CTR RT), Eric Isselée/SS; 65, Rob Nelson @UntamedScience; 65 (UP RT), GarysFRP/GI; 65 (LO LE), Visuals Unlimited, Inc./Nigel Cattlin/GI; 66 (UP), Jelger Herder/Buiten-beeld/MP; 66 (CTR), Lovely Bird/SS; 66 (LO), Juan Gaertner/SS; 66 (LO LE), Simon Shim/SS; 66-67, John Wollwerth/SS; 67 (UP), Maksimilian/SS; 67 (UP RT), Joel Sartore, National Geographic Photo Ark/National Geographic Image Collection; 67 (CTR RT), Melinda Fawver/SS; 67 (LO RT), mcmac/SS; 68 (UP), Visual Generation/SS; 68 (LO), Viorika Klotz/EyeEm/GI; 69, Lorenz and Avelar/GI; **Chapter 5:** 70-71, Pete Oxford/MP; 72, Photo Researchers/GI; 73 (CTR), NOAA; 74, Konrad Wothe/MP; 74 (LO), Auscape/GI; 75, Stephen Ausmus/U.S. Department of Agriculture/Science Photo Library; 75 (LO), Stephen Ausmus/U.S. Department of Agriculture/Science Photo Library; 76 (UP), Ed Reschke/GI; 76 (CTR), Henri Koskinen/SS; 76 (LO LE), NK-55/SS; 76 (LO), Robert Young/EyeEm/GI; 77, Joel Sartore, National Geographic Photo Ark/NGC; 77 (LO), PJF Military Collection/Alamy; 78, MikeLane45/GI; 78 (LO), Michael and Patricia Fogden/MP; 79, Ron Winkler; 80 (UP), Sebastian Kennerknecht/MP; 80 (LO), Peter Blackwell/NPL/MP; 81 (UP), Tom Vezo/MP; 81 (CTR), Tim Fitzharris/MP; 81 (LO), Vagner Reis Reis/EyeEm/GI; 82 (UP), Layne Kennedy/GI; 82 (LO), William Campbell/Sygma via GI; 82-83, Ronan Donovan/NGC; 83 (LO), Layne Kennedy/GI; 84, Frank Glaw; 84 (LO), Frank Glaw; 85, Martin Willis/MP; 85 (RT), Rosl Roessner/BIA/MP/MP; 86 (LO), Paul Starosta/GI; 86 (UP), Gregory S. Paulson/GI; 87 (UP), 3Dstock/SS; 88 (LO), PhotoBarmaley/SS; 88-89, J.C. Dollman/Ivy Close Images/AGE Fotostock; 89 (LO), THEPALMER/GI; **End matter:** 90-91, Matthew Cicanese; 92 (LO), Rich Carey/SS; 92 (UP), Cristi180884/Dreamstime; 93 (UP LE), Eric Isselée/SS; 93 (UP RT), Olga Bogatyrenko/SS; 94 (LO) Anand Varma/NGC; 96 (UP), Jay Ondreicka/SS

INDEX

Boldface indicates illustrations.

EURASIAN
EAGLE-OWL

Since 1888, the National Geographic Society
has funded more than 12,000 research, explo-
ration, and preservation projects around
the world. The Society receives funds from
National Geographic Partners, LLC, funded
in part by your purchase. A portion of the
proceeds from this book supports this vital
work. To learn more, visit natgeo.com/info.

For more information, visit national
geographic.com, call 1-800-647-5463,
or write to the following address:

National Geographic Partners
1145 17th Street N.W.
Washington, D.C. 20036-4688 U.S.A.

Visit us online at nationalgeographic.com/
books

For librarians and teachers:
ngchildrensbooks.org

More for kids from National Geographic:
natgeokids.com

For information about special discounts
for bulk purchases, please contact
National Geographic Books Special Sales:
specialsales@natgeo.com

For rights or permissions inquiries,
please contact National Geographic
Books Subsidiary Rights:
bookrights@natgeo.com

Designed by Callie Broaddus

The publisher would like to thank Paige
Towler, project editor; Shannon Hibberd,
photo editor; Christina Ascani, photo
editor; Anne LeongSon and Gus Tello,
production assistants; and Jennifer
Kelly Geddes, fact-checker.

Library of Congress Cataloging-in-Publication
Data

Names: Stiefel, Chana, author. | National
  Geographic Society (U.S.)
Title: Animal zombies!/by Chana Steifel.
  Description: Washington, DC : National
  Geographic Kids, [2018] | Audience: Ages
  8-12. | Audience: Grades 4 to 6. |
  Includes index.
Identifiers: LCCN 2017050030|
  ISBN 9781426331497 (pbk.) |
  ISBN 9781426331503 (hardcover)
Subjects: LCSH: Parasites--Behavior--
  Juvenile literature. | Parasitism--Juvenile
  literature. | Animal behavior--Juvenile
  literature.
Classification: LCC QL757 .S74 2018 |
  DDC 577.8/57--dc23
LC record available at
  https://lccn.loc.gov/2017050030

Printed in China
18/RRDH/1